THE GIFT HALF UNDERSTOOD
essays on a European journey

Alastair Hulbert

For Fiona, Estyn and Garth

THE GIFT HALF UNDERSTOOD

essays on a European journey

Alastair Hulbert

MELISENDE

The Gift Half Understood
by Alastair Hulbert

First published 2002
by Melisende
39 Chelmsford Road
London E18 2PW
Tel: 020 8498 9768
Fax: 020 8504 2558
e-mail: melisende@cwcom.net
www. melisende.cwc.net

ISBN 1 901 764 11 7

Edited by Leonard Harrow

Printed in England by the St Edmundsbury Press

Contents

Preface

Some time ago, when I began putting this book together out of all the funny bits and pieces I have collected over the years, I imagined that what I was doing was editing a travel journal, or was it writing essays in geography, or making poetry, or even doing theology? To tell the truth, I wasn't quite sure what I was doing. With time, however, I have come to realise that what I am searching for is a sense of place, and a celebration of the beauty and diversity of Europe as it faces further unification and the shocks of globalisation.

One of the consequences of globalisation is that the rootedness in time and place which has served to anchor culture and meaning in ages past is being undermined. The globalised, technocratic powers which are taking over the world (large corporations, financial institutions, advertising agencies, tourism) are taking off—like a kind of cultural B52 bomber, practically invisible and devastatingly indiscriminate in their impact. Remember Vietnam and the Gulf War. The Royal Dutch/Shell Group is such a corporation. As I say in one of the essays, it calls its strategic perspective on the future TINA: There Is No Alternative—no alternative, that is, to Shell's own style of multinational, technocratic capitalism.

I beg to differ. Reading Dostoevsky's *The Idiot* again has reminded me of the Orthodox association of beauty with salvation: Beauty Will Save The World. (Maybe we should call it BWSTW for short.) But it's not just any kind of beauty that will save the world. The reason why Prince Myshkin believes that beauty will save the world, according to his young friend Ippolit, is that he is in love. And Ippolit himself is dying of consumption.

What sort of beauty, charged with love, will save the world? Surely it cannot be the beauty of Warsaw's Lazienki Park with its palaces and peacocks, or the Winged Victory of Samothrace, plucked from its Aegean island, to dominate a staircase in the Louvre. Rather is it the beauty of a Creator who, chiding his own forgetfulness, throws all his remaining jewels out of the window—to create the Hebrides; or a consuming passion as in the words, 'I would gladly die for the Madonna of Wrocław.'

My wife and I have lived and worked on the continent for much of the last thirty years. The essays in the first and third parts of the book draw on this background. During the 1990s I was seconded by the Church of Scotland to an office in Brussels representing the European churches in their relations with the European Union. One of my tasks was to return to Scotland from time to time on deputation, visiting different parts of the country, presenting European affairs and the work of the churches to presbyteries and congregations, schools and groups of all sorts, and listening to their views in return. The essays in Part Two result from some of these Scottish visits. The shape of the book is intended to reinforce a sense of Scotland in Europe and Scottish–European identity.

I wish to express my gratitude to the World Mission Department of the Church of Scotland for all their encouragement and support, including financial, with the book. My warm thanks also go to the Margaret Fraser and Robert Mackie Fund, and to the Drummond Trust, 3 Pitt Terrace, Stirling, for financial assistance in the publication of the book.

Thanks especially to Fiona, my wife, who appears as part of my 'we' in several of the essays. Without her help in so many ways the book would not have appeared. And thanks to Estyn and Garth who lived so many of our European years with us.

Edinburgh
Easter, 2001

Part One

To show where the secret was found

> ... These are only hints and guesses,
> Hints followed by guesses; and the rest
> Is prayer, observance, discipline, thought and action.
> The hint half guessed, the gift half understood, is Incarnation.
> T S Eliot, *Four Quartets, The Dry Salvages.*

*   *   *

> ... hoping to find some secret. A secret not about art, but about life. And if one finds one, it remains a secret, because, finally, it is untranslatable into words. With words one can only, sometimes, make a clumsy map, hand-drawn, to show where the secret was found.
> John Berger, *The infinity of desire.*

Vilnius

Can art save the world?

*I challenge you all now, all you atheists. With what will you save
the world, and where have you found a normal line of progress for
it, you men of science, of industry, of co-operation, of labour-
wage, and all the rest of it? With what? With credit? What's
credit? Where will credit take you?*

Dostoevsky, *The Idiot*

It must be unusual for an art exhibition to be opened by two state
presidents together, and rather extraordinary too for there to be only
one painting on show. But this was no usual exhibition and no ordinary
painting.

Jan Matejko's vast canvas, *The Battle of Tannenberg* (4.26 x
9.87 metres), was completed in 1878, and had already done the rounds
of half the capitals of Europe by the end of the nineteenth century.
Today it is the best-loved painting in the Polish National Gallery and
still goes on tour. Its subject is one of the greatest battles of mediaeval
Europe, when the united Lithuanian and Polish armies took on the
knights of the Teutonic Order, the Order of the Cross, in 1410 and
defeated them, thus heralding the end of two centuries of the German
Crusaders' domination of the Baltic region. During World War II, the
Nazis realised the painting's political significance and power but, like a
member of the resistance, it was already in hiding, and they searched
for it in vain.

The exhibition was in Vilnius, in the museum of the former
Arsenal of the Lower Castle, and was inaugurated by the Presidents
of both Lithuania and Poland. The importance of its message for
modern Lithuania, still waking up after another of its dark nights of
the soul, justified not only the show itself but also the political presence.

The picture captures the decisive moment of the battle of
Tannenberg, near Gdansk, when the Grand Master of the Teutonic
Knights, Ulrich von Jungingen, is being set upon by the two foot
soldiers, Lithuanian and Polish, who brought him down. His death
was the turning point of the battle. Nearby, in the midst of a seething

mass of fighting men, the Lithuanian Grand Duke Vytautas, eyes ablaze, a heroic figure in scarlet on a galloping horse, provides the very image of victory. King Vladislav Jagellon, Vytautas's cousin and ally, watches the battle from the distance in the top right hand corner of the canvas.

In Warsaw, *The Battle of Tannenberg* normally occupies a commanding position in the National Gallery on the end wall of the wing that houses its nineteenth century collection. In Vilnius, it was hung in the Arsenal in such a way as to dominate the perspective in a long and airy gallery with little else to distract the attention. Groups of school children and busloads of ordinary citizens from far and wide approached it like pilgrims approaching a shrine.

Another monumental historical work by Jan Matejko, *Sobieski liberates Vienna* (4.58 x 8.94 metres), was presented by the artist himself to Pope Leo XIII on the occasion of the bicentenary of the defeat of the Turks in 1683. It gives its name to the Sobieski Room in the Vatican museum where it hangs. The victory of Christian Europe over Islam may be less topical today when there is a growing dialogue with Muslims, than the victory of Tannenberg as the Baltic States celebrate independence from Russia, yet both paintings still carry powerful messages, not only about the past, but also about the present and future.

Matejko was a native of Cracow and he painted both masterpieces there. How many hours, I wonder, has the former Archbishop of Cracow spent in the Sobieski Room in the Vatican, meditating on his cherished ideas of a Christian Europe—as he must have been inspired by Raphael's Sala Della Signatura a few rooms away for his belief in the central control of the papacy. It's hard to imagine anywhere else in the world where, in so contained a space, raw earthly power is transfigured with such exquisite taste and beauty.

To celebrate its year as European City of Culture in 1993, Antwerp published a poster of Manet's *The Fifer* with the question, 'Can art save the world?' The choice of painting was deliberately provocative. Plucked from the art critical quarrels of nineteenth century France, Manet's *Fifer* shows a Parisian street urchin portrayed as if he were a Spanish grandee, a young bandsman of the light-infantry in a uniform of red and black and gold, looking straight at the spectator like a saint out of a stained glass window. But on a monochrome background of luminous grey, with no context and no perspective, as if the boy is surrounded by nothing but air.[1]

How does art relate to its context and surroundings? the poster seems to be asking—either technically within the painting, or beyond the canvas in the real world. Surely art cannot save the world—out of the blue, out of luminous grey!

In his history of Europe Norman Davies analyses a painting by the Soviet artist Alexei Vasilev.[2] It is called *They are talking about us in Pravda.* Five young agricultural workers are sitting in a field eating their lunch on a rug with a pattern which suggests that the scene is in Moldavia. The stubble field, golden in the sunlight, stretches away to a broad valley with wooded hills beyond. In the distance a combine harvester is still at work, while nearby a motorcycle is parked. One of the group, a girl in a coloured headscarf, is reading from the newspaper while her comrades look on smiling. It may not be great art but the overall effect is pleasing enough.

As Davies points out, all the characteristics of Socialist Realism are represented in the picture: national spirit, devotion to the party, class-consciousness, ideological character, representative message. Yet in fact, none of what is portrayed was true. Soviet Communism had destroyed Moldavia's traditional culture, its population had been purged and the peasantry collectivised by force. In the painting 'all the most important realities of life ... have been systematically falsified.'

Socialist Realism is now a backwater in art history because it had a romantic revolutionary purpose which was supposed to contribute to saving the world, but in reality tended to just the opposite. Davies ends his reflections with this poignant question, 'How much aesthetic value can art retain when, in human and moral terms, its principal purpose is fraudulent?'

*   *   *

Our friends, Gia and Yanina, were so proud of their new Vilnius, fast fulfilling its designs for renovation. An astonishing amount of rebuilding has been completed in less than a decade, though there's so much still to be done. There are forty churches in the old town of Vilnius.

---

[1] *Manet 1832-1883*, Éditions de la Réunion des musées nationaux, Paris, 1983, pp. 243-247.

[2] Norman Davies, *Europe: a history*, Oxford University Press, 1996, p. 1011.

Voluptuous baroque facades are newly painted in the lovely white and pastel colours of the originals. They say that Vilnius had the most concentrated collection of baroque buildings outside Brazil! And like Brazil, it had the Jesuits to thank for it. But there is St Anne's as well, a beautiful gothic church. It so enraptured Napoleon during his Russian campaign that he longed to take it home with him—if only he were God, he is reported to have said, in the palm of his hand!

The Lutheran church, where Yanina invited us to celebrate Pentecost with Gia and other friends, is in a courtyard off one of the central avenues of the city. It has been beautifully restored with help from the church in Germany. Until a decade ago, and during the half century when Lithuania was under the Soviet Union, it was a sports hall, while the nearby Catholic Church of St Cazimir, the oldest church in Vilnius, was a museum of atheism. Today there were old and young at the service. Lunch followed in the church house across the courtyard, and afterwards someone sat down to play the accordion and people began to dance. There was a lot of laughter. The memories of an all too recent, painful past, it seemed, made celebrating the gift of the Holy Spirit to the church at Pentecost a welcome thing to do.

Just down the road is the Lithuanian National Gallery. It is housed in a refurbished palace in the heart of old Vilnius. The collection is mainly of religious art and eighteenth-nineteenth century oil painting. To be frank, I found it difficult to appreciate much of it. But one little oil painting caught me by surprise. It was called *Through the Rye,* and the artist's name was Juozapas Balzukevicius (1866-1915).

Three peasants, two women wearing headscarves and shawls and a man with a long coat, dark cap and staff, are walking away, along a path which disappears in a shoulder high field of rye. The sky fills nearly half the picture with a bank of cloud—a play of light and shadow with whites, touched with ochres, blues and greys. The rye field has the many shades of amber, the gold of the north. The countryside is flat as far as the eye can see. On the low horizon is the hazy outline of a city with domes and towers, and a great church. Some way in front of the three travellers, almost hidden by the rye, is another figure, who, from his black coat and wide-brimmed hat, is a Jew. Vilnius had 104 synagogues at one time; its ghetto earned it the name, 'Jerusalem of the East'.

Our bus journey home across western Lithuania and the great north-eastern plains of Poland was pure celebration. Vilnius, Trakai,

Alytus, Augustów, Grajewo, Lomza, Warsaw—and mile upon mile of the lean road through lush grasslands, brilliant with dandelions. Forests, where the sun lit up the tiny leaves and loose bark of birch trees, and highlighted the ruddy trunks of pines against the dark green needles of their branches. Past lots of little lakes with reeds and rushes round their edges. Faded yellow clapboard cottages, with suddenly, mysteriously, a stork gliding overhead. Lilac and hawthorn and rowan in bloom.

When Ivan Illich ended his essay, *The Powerless Church*,[3] about the role of the church in social change, with the words, 'I want to celebrate my faith for no purpose at all', he was seeking to restore a faith which association with power had put in jeopardy. What he wanted was something quite different from the kind of theological justification of social action which is easy to come by. He wished to leave room for people to be surprised by faith, at a remove from the reasons which motivate social action.

'All men experience life—,' Illich wrote, 'the Christian believes he has discovered its meaning … like the laughter in the joke.' He was not deploring social action—far from it. His point was that the modern humanist does not need to rely on the gospel as a norm for social action. Secular ideology can assume that task.

I think it's the same with art.

---

[3] In Ivan D Illich, *Celebration of Awareness*, Calder & Boyers, London, 1971, pp. 95-103.

Cordoba
The only way of salvation

There is in the history of Europe a latent theology of religions.
Europe has had confidence in herself. Her conduct, for good as for
ill, can be explained thanks to a theologoumenon: Christianity is
the one totally true religion, the only way of salvation.[1]

Santiago, St James, is the patron saint of Spain. He is called James
Major in the tradition to distinguish him from Jesus' brother James,
James Minor. The son of Zebedee and brother of John, he and Peter
and John were Jesus' closest friends. They were all present at the
Transfiguration and in Gethsemane. James preached the Gospel in
what is now called the West Bank and was the first disciple to be
martyred. According to tradition he was beheaded.

By the time of the Crusades, the site of the Armenian
Cathedral of St James in Jerusalem was venerated as the place where
James's head was buried. But from the seventh century it was maintained
that he also preached in Spain, and from the ninth his body was believed
to have emerged miraculously in a stone sarcophagus out of the Atlantic
Ocean at Compostela in Galicia. It was then that Santiago de Compostela
became one of the most popular places of pilgrimage in mediaeval
Europe.

At the end of the Middle Ages the Catholic sovereigns called
on Santiago's help to expel the Moors from Spain. He fought on their
side as *Matamoros*, Hammer of the Moors. Then the Conquistadores
conscripted him to invade the New World with them, and he earned
the title *Mataindios*, Hammer of the Indians, leaving behind a terrible
legacy of conquest. Santiago de los Caballeros was founded in the
Dominican Republic in 1494 by Christopher Columbus, Santiago de
Cuba in 1514, in 1541 Santiago de Chile—del Nuevo Extremo (of the
new frontier), whose Araucanian name had been Huelen, meaning
'pain'—Santiago del Estero in north-west Argentina in 1553, Santiago

---

[1] Raimon Panikkar, *1492-1992—Conquète et évangile en Amérique Latine: Questions pour l'Europe*
aujourd'hui, Actes du Colloque réalisé à Lyon du 28 au 30 janvier 1992 à l'Université
Catholique de Lyon, p. 42, my translation.

de la Vega in Jamaica, Santiago de Surco near Lima in Peru, the Rio Grande de Santiago on the Pacific side of Mexico, Nicaragua's Santiago volcano, and so on and on. 'During the tough years of the conquest the clash of arms was heard from the tomb of Santiago in Compostela on the eve of each battle; and the apostle fought with the invading hosts, lance in hand, on his white horse.'[2]

*   *   *

Cordoba's vast sixteenth century cathedral squats incongruously within the sanctuary of Europe's largest mosque, built over a thousand years ago. The imposition of the cathedral's soaring vaults with their feeling for infinity on the earthy horizontal rhythm of the mosque's arcades is a unique religious and architectural impropriety. Even so fervent a Catholic as the Emperor Charles V is reported to have remarked, 'You have built here what you or anyone might have built anywhere else, but you have destroyed what is unique in the world.'

On the north side of the cathedral nave there is a baroque statue, unnoticed in the guidebooks, which portrays a cavalier with wide-brimmed hat and swept-back cape, sword raised as his rampant horse tramples a turbaned Moor. When I protested to a passing guardian of the holy place at such a blatant image of Santiago Matamoros, he would have none of it, insisting that it was Santiago Apostolos! More than any other European saint or symbol down the ages, St James epitomizes Panikkar's theologoumenon: Christianity is the one totally true religion, the only way of salvation.

In spite of this it is no longer correct or fashionable in Spain—or indeed anywhere else in Europe—to speak in terms of Christian superiority. Even a declaration of Pope John Paul II, on a commemorative plaque behind the cathedral choir dated 21 June 1985, proclaims 'The celebration of the XII centenary [of the mosque] offers a propitious occasion to manifest the fraternity between men who profess their faith in the one God.' This is a nice, chummy statement by the holy father but, with no reference to the past, it means little.

The Roger Garaudy Foundation which has its seat in the Calahorra Tower, the ancient Moorish bastion built to defend Cordoba's Roman bridge over the Guadalquivir, elegantly portrays the case for

---

[2] Eduardo Galeano, *Memory of Fire*, Vol. I, *Genesis*, Quartet Books, London, 1985, p. 151.

inter-religious tolerance and cooperation in a 'heritage experience' entitled *De cómo el hombre se convirtió en humano*. The Cordoba of the Caliphate, 'the ornament of the world' as the Saxon poet Hroswitha called it, where once a million people lived in harmony in Europe's largest city, is celebrated as a bridge between East and West, a symbol of cohabitation between the three monotheistic religions. 'From the first Moslem Friday service pronounced in the Mosque in 788, to the first Catholic mass celebrated there on 19 June 1236, and through all the different liturgies, this monument continues to be inhabited by the same God.' But such talk of the golden age of Andalusia is really little more than sentimentality if no mention is made of the terrible religious conflict that dominated other periods.

Only the Arabic inscription above the Mihrab, the empty niche which indicates the way to face for prayer, shows any real ecumenical intention. 'Believer,' it reads, 'whatever thy faith, let this sheaf of splendour and fire grow within thee.' For Muslims beauty is one of the signs which evoke God's presence and the mihrab is adorned with beautiful airy mosaic decorations to encourage believers.

The circumstance which has made it politically incorrect in Europe today to preach Christian superiority is that culturally it doesn't matter any more. It doesn't make any difference. During the three hundred years that Cordoba was the seat of the Inquisition, as long as the church and Christianity provided the controlling, organisational principle for European society, it mattered. But since that time, Europe and the West have in fact been moving towards another kind of social supremacy—economic, technocratic culture. The archetype is the same.

The Islamism of recent years is a reaction to this new form of Western supremacy. Tarek Mitri writes, 'Islam's bursting onto the political scene is often perceived as a step backwards, a medieval anachronism, an onslaught on modernity: *but it's not the Middle Ages that are resurfacing in our time; it is modernism that is secreting its own forms of protest* ... Sociologically speaking, the Islamist movements are a product of the modern world.'[3] Fundamentalism is a way of standing up to the hegemony of modernism with its liberal economics and technocratic culture.

---

[3] Tarek Mitri, 'Islam, Modernity and Islamism' in Mohammed Arkoun and Tarek Mitri, *Islam, Europe and Modernity*, ed. Alastair Hulbert, AOES Occasional Paper No. 2, Brussels, 1996, p. 5, 7.

* * *

It was springtime and there was enough water in the Guadalquivir—the 'great river' (*wadi al kibir*)—to cover its wide river bed. A fig tree at the end of the ancient Roman bridge was laden with young figs. Jackdaws were in and out of holes in the embankment wall. Dippers with clean white bibs danced on the rocks and in the weed around the fourteen pillars of the bridge. A dilapidated stone building on an island and the ancient Arab irrigation wheel by the bank gave the place a sense of outdistanced conviviality. The run-down Hostal Mari by the mosque where I was staying had a young Moroccan proprietor called Mohammed. Cordoba suited him, he told me. I could imagine that. Cordoba may be 'the bridge from East to West', but the old city felt more like East than West to me. There were many Moroccans in the city. Mohammed managed to make ends meet and nobody bothered him much. So no, he didn't expect to return home except on holiday.

March is the time to visit Cordoba. It's like the best days of summer in the north. I spent a while in the souk going back and forth between shops and stalls to select matching Andalusian pottery with a Moorish design as a gift for my daughter. The statue of a seated Maimonides, in a corner of the Jewish quarter with its whitewashed alleyways and leafy patios, was what I remembered best from an earlier visit. As I made my way up the Calle Jesus y Maria towards the Viana Palace, college students of the Escuele Superior de Arte Dramatico y Danza were lounging around in the street: pretty girls tightly packed into their jeans and sweaters, beautiful dark-haired boys.

The twelve courtyards, the fountains and gardens of the fifteenth century Viana Palace is the nearest Cordoba gets to Granada's incomparable Alhambra. In its galleries a life-sized, full-length portrait of General Franco—supremo in the mould of Santiago's shadow side—is simply ignored by the guides. It still hangs where it has hung for over half a century, alongside eighteenth century tapestries woven to the young Goya's cartoons of peasant life.

The Julio Romero de Torres Museum in the Plazuela del Potro houses paintings of sultry women, madonnas and prostitutes. Across the road still stands the inn which Don Quixote took for a castle, and where, at the beginning of his story, he persuaded the innkeeper, whom he took for the warden of the castle, to confer his knighthood on him.

A sweeper was sweeping the dusty beaten earth of the footpath outside the Alcázar when I arrived. The gardens were alive with the sound of running water. Along a wide corridor, marble-paved, and up a little flight of stairs there is a room which looks out over the castle courtyard. It's called the *Salon del Océano*. In it is a table with a tabletop of wooden marquetry representing the map painted in 1500 by Juan de la Cosa, Columbus's Basque pilot—the first map of the New World. The original is in Madrid. A wind rose in mid-Atlantic carries a portrait of the Virgin, while at the western edge of the map, covering the eastern coastline of Central America, is a miniature icon of St Christopher and the Christ child. He represents Christopher Columbus of course, carrying Christendom across the ocean to America.

The sense of mission was a powerful but short-lived influence in the main thrust of the discoveries. No subsequent map of the New World figures the Christ in this way. There were other, weightier reasons for Europe's outreach and expansion—trade routes to discover, commerce, plunder, and the lust for gold and silver. The fact that the arrangements which led to the 'discovery' of America were agreed between Columbus and *los Reyes Catholicos* in Cordoba, in what had once been the capital of the Moorish kingdom, underlines the continuity between the *Reconquista* (of Spain) and the *Conquista* (of the Americas). The one ended in January 1492; the other began in October 1492.

Spain was at the height of its powers when Christopher Columbus broke out of the confines of Christendom on to the world stage. '1492 is the first "European" date in world history, and from this point the "centrality" of Europe was slowly constructed in the sixteenth century.'[4] Columbus's voyages of discovery may have been an amazing feat, not only in terms of science and technology, but also of courage. But on the occasion of the five hundredth anniversary of the event, in spite of Spain's extravagant celebrations of the discoveries and of itself as a member of the European Union and the world community following the end of Francismo—Seville as host to Expo 92, Madrid as the European City of Culture, and Barcelona hosting the Olympics—it failed to recognise and come to terms with the deeper meaning and significance of 1492.

In 1992 the first museum of the Holocaust on German soil was inaugurated to mark fifty years since the Wansee Conference in

---

[4] Enrique Dussel, 'The Real Motives for the Conquest, 1492-1992', in *The Voice of the Victims*, ed. Leonardo Boff and Virgil Elizondo, *Concilium 1990/6*, SCM Press, London, p. 33.

Berlin defined the Nazi policy which exterminated six million Jews. It took long enough. 1992 offered a unique opportunity to create a lasting memorial in Seville, Madrid or even Brussels to what was by far the greatest genocide in human history, perpetrated by Christendom (Europe) on the new world. Modern studies calculate the indigenous population of Latin America and the Caribbean in 1492 at 100 million people. By 1570 the terrifying truth is that only 10-12 million were left.[5]

To Europeans, America was a new world, giving access to untold wealth. To the indigenous population it was the world of always, and it ended. What Bartolomé de las Casas wrote about the murder of Moctezuma applies to Latin America as a whole: 'This was something which threw all these kingdoms and peoples into grief and anguish and mourning and pain... and from now to the end of the world, or they die out completely, they will not cease to lament ...' Spain and the European Union missed the chance of a century to make symbolic recognition of it in 1992.

In the gardens of Cordoba's Alcázar, between the orange groves and fountains stands a statue of Christopher Columbus meeting Ferdinand and Isabella. The orange trees were laden with ripe Seville oranges, the ground strewn with fallen fruit. I gathered three large oranges and stuffed them into my satchel. Back home in Brussels I cooked them with coarse cane sugar from the Americas to make marmalade, a dark gold, bitter-sweet confection with which to greet the day.

---

[5] Pablo Richard, '1492: The Violence of God and the Future of Christianity', *op. cit.*, p. 59.

Graz
How do we escape from history?

And a great portent appeared in heaven, a woman clothed with the sun, with the moon under her feet, and on her head a crown of twelve stars; she was with child and she cried out in her pangs of birth, in anguish for delivery. And another portent appeared in heaven; behold a great red dragon ...
Revelation 12: 1-3.

With chapter twelve of the drama of Revelation, the end time of struggle with the Antichrist begins. The author of the Apocalypse, whether he was John the beloved disciple of Jesus or not, wrote like a 'son of thunder', indignant with the enemies of his Lord, eager to destroy them and sit at the Messiah's right hand in glory. It was an obvious theological exercise for the Jesuits to translate such first century imagery—Jewish and Christian, borrowing also from Greek, Egyptian, even Persian mythology—into the political context of sixteenth century central Europe.

The old town of Graz is full of representations of this woman, brightly gilded, standing on a sickle moon, a crown of twelve stars around her head, a snake beneath her feet. The dragon of Revelation has been fused with the serpent of Genesis 3, as the woman was deliberately incorporated into the images of Eve and the Virgin Mary. The baroque statue on the north wall of the choir of the city's Franziskanerkirche is the richest and most exquisite of these representations of Mariology, though it doesn't go so far as to have her carrying a child with a cross, as does the statue on a pillar in the nave of Antwerp Cathedral, nor associate her with the dogma of the immaculate conception, as does a painting of her by Vélasquez in the National Gallery of London.

In the second half of the sixteenth century, Graz was the capital of Inner Austria, a vast area of the Hapsburg domains including Styria, Carinthia, Gorizia, Carniola and Istria. For two whole centuries, from 1480 until 1683, the Turkish threat hung over the valley of the

Mur, which flows deep and swiftly through the old city. The Mur and the Drava, the Enns and the Sann—rivers of Styria at the time of the Hapsburgs and represented by four female statues round the fountain in the Hauptplatz—are all drawn towards the East, flowing into the Danube. Although the Mur at Graz is only a hundred and fifty miles from Venice and the Adriatic, its waters pour into the Black Sea seven hundred and fifty miles away.

But the dragon, the serpent, the devil, for sixteenth century Catholicism, was the Reformation. By 1568 three-quarters of the population of Graz was Protestant. The new humanism flourished. Kepler, the German astronomer, taught here. In 1571, the Archduke Charles II called in the Jesuits, as elsewhere in Central Europe, to rid the land of the reformed faith. The Company of Jesus was the most businesslike and efficient order the Catholic church has ever produced. With its military model, its manual of Christian warfare in the *Spiritual Exercises* of Ignatius, its alternative hierarchy and Roman ecclesiastical authority, its educational control through schools and universities for the well-born and well-to-do, you couldn't deny its effectiveness. No more than a handful of Protestants survived. Graz is a testimony to the success of the Counter-Reformation. And all in honour of the woman of Revelation 12: 1-3! As if in premonition of what his followers would suffer in its name, Martin Luther didn't like the Book of Revelation. And more recently theologians have acknowledged that the God of the Apocalypse can hardly be recognised as the father of our Lord Jesus Christ.

Alongside banners celebrating the Second European Ecumenical Assembly above the entrance of the elegant nineteenth century city hall, a simpler representation of Revelation 12:1-3 dominated the Hauptplatz of Graz in June 1997—as if there were no connection: twelve gold stars on a blue ground—the flag of modern Europe, as adopted by the Council of Europe in 1955, and the European Community thirty years later.

Graz, the 'green heart' of Austria, was never a border town until the redivision of Europe in 1918. The imperial history, the stately houses, the baroque churches, the fruit dumplings, are all central European. Lookout points on the Schlossberg in the middle of the town indicate the direction and the distance to all the capitals of Europe (except Brussels). On the opening day of the European Ecumenical Assembly, in one two hour period some four thousand participants

23

(out of a total of over ten thousand) arrived in two trains that had journeyed for a day and a half from Moscow and from Bucharest, taking travellers on board all along the way from Tallinn and Vilnius, Warsaw and Prague, Bratislava and Budapest, and many other places in the countries these capitals represent. The European Christians gathering in Graz in response to a call for reconciliation were a reminder in the multitude of their arrivals of that other massive assembly of Europeans but with a dreadful, necrophilic intention over fifty years ago. The reception in the Hauptbahnhof of Graz was no doubt more chaotic than the sidings of the concentration camp in Auschwitz, the arrivals here were restricted to one day. But the glimpse of this other town at the heart of Europe—at a railway junction and a crossroads, with such a radically transformed vocation for the old continent— was moving and salutary.

The spacious third-floor apartment on the Hauptplatz of Graz, near the great mediaeval mural of St Christopher dominating the square, which served as the local office of the Ecumenical Assembly for over a year, was the Gestapo's headquarters during the war. Its operations room had a swastika as the centrepiece of the polished parquet floor. Now, it housed a European initiative for 'reconciliation, gift of God and source of new life'.

At dusk the great tethered banners (red and white for Austria, green and white for Styria), flanking the clock tower on the Schlossberg, flap loudly, urgently, in the rising wind, as in a Kurosawa film about mediaeval warfare. Not just the Jesuits, but the Turks, Napoleon, Hitler—all passed this way. And what a crossroads Europe is at again!

'Oh, the great chaos of this continent,' cries Starhemberg, an imperial general in Howard Barker's play, *The Europeans*, 'The beating of lives in the bowl of obscure quarrels, the batter of perpetual and necessary horror ... How do we escape from History? We reproduce its mayhem in our lives ...'[1] The scene is not far away, outside the walls of Vienna, the occasion the enemy's rape and mutilation of a young woman and the fate of her infant child, the date 1683 and the defeat of the Turks by Jan Sobieski, King of Poland. Nearby such barbarism has returned in recent times. Graz was chosen for the Ecumenical Assembly because of its proximity to Bosnia-Herzegovina.

---

[1] Howard Barker, *The Europeans: Struggles to Love*, John Calder, London, 1990, pp. 44-45.

Next to the Sobieski Room in the Vatican is the Room of the Immaculate Conception, its cabinets packed with ornate volumes in many languages proclaiming the papal bull of the dogma of the origins of the virgin. Oh, what this culture does with its women—what it has done with the handmaid of the Lord, the annunciation, the time of waiting for the gift of God! No twelve-star crown she wore. Her son bore a crown of thorns.

Here ends the known

*Now. When I have overcome my fear—of others, of myself, of the
underlying darkness; at the frontier of the unheard-of.*
*Here ends the known. But, from a source beyond it,
something fills my being with its possibilities.*[1]

It was Dag Hammarskjöld who, as secretary general of the United
Nations, created a *lieu de recueillement* or meditation room in the UN
headquarters in New York. He wanted to set aside a place to which
people could withdraw during the working day, to reflect and
reconstitute themselves for the task in hand. He sought to nurture
spiritual awareness and vitality, long before the need for spirituality
was expressed as strongly as it is today. Hammarskjöld's intimate journal,
Markings, published after his death, was his own personal *lieu de
recueillement*, accompanying him on his travels. He once described it in
diplomatic terms as 'a sort of *White Paper* concerning my negotiations
with myself—and with God.'

With the construction of the Berlaymont in Brussels, that
great symbol of the European Communities built in the shape of a
star or a cross, the European Commission established its own *lieu de
recueillement*. It was a suite of two rooms under the Rue de la Loi,
opposite the main entrance to the Commission headquarters, on the
other side of the little forest of cherry trees which used to so illumine
the courtyard in April with their dense, pink blossoms. The French
verb *se recueillir* means to collect one's thoughts, to commune with
oneself, to be plunged in meditation. *Lieu de recueillement* means a place
of quiet, conducive to meditation or prayer, a meditation centre.
Officials in the administration tend to employ the French term, rather
than the English.

The *lieu de recueillement* always belonged to the secular, public
institution of the European Commission. But, quite remarkably,
responsibility for its use was conferred on two church bodies, the
European Catholic Centre on the one hand, and the Ecumenical

---

[1] Dag Hammarskjöld, *Markings*, Faber & Faber, London, 1964, p. 77.

Association for Church and Society, an association of civil servants, on the other. Openness and availability to everyone associated with the European civil service, regardless of philosophy or creed, were the only conditions. When the Berlaymont closed for refurbishment in 1992, the *lieu de recueillement* was transferred to an office block down the road, where a large room divided up into chapel, lecture hall and kitchen, offers a meeting place for reflection, worship and debate. The musicians' circle of the Commission also uses it for concerts.

Not far away, near the Grande Place, the mediaeval Church of St Nicholas is still surrounded by tiny houses and shops, luckenbooths, leaning against its sturdy walls. Elsewhere in Europe— St Bavo's Cathedral in Gent for example, St Giles' in Edinburgh— such ancient lean-tos have been demolished in an effort to tidy up the cathedral's surroundings. Here they preserve the symbolism of a church that lives with and for the people.

The *lieu de recueillement* is situated now in the heart of an EC tower block, surrounded by corridors and offices, committee rooms, cafeteria and car park. It has no windows, only skylights, some candles, a bare wooden cross and, on the wall, a copy of Rublev's icon of the Holy Trinity. It may be less beautiful, but as a symbol, it is no less compelling than St Nicholas's. Constituted as an empty space within a complex administration, it bears witness to something else, the Other, beyond the limits of the institutions of government. 'Here ends the known.'

Like the years we are living through now, the Renaissance was a period of enormous energy and imagination. But the sailors and explorers of what has also been called the 'age of reconnaissance',[2] were in fact groping their way around the world. Technically they could manage well enough—though many were shipwrecked and lost in the process—but they were quite unaware of the dimensions of what was out there. On his first voyage of discovery, beyond the relative safety of European or African coastal waters, beyond the circle of ocean on the periphery of the *mappa mundi*, beyond the known, Christopher Columbus regularly falsified the ship's log, reducing the number of leagues covered each day, 'so as not to terrify the crew', as he wrote in his report to Ferdinand and Isabella.

---

[2] J H Parry, *The Age of Reconnaissance*, Weidenfeld and Nicolson, London, 1963.

Following the end of the Cold War and the collapse of the Soviet empire, Europe is again undergoing enormous changes. In 1989 there was a surge of enthusiasm and a sense of purpose; but as the century ends there is great uncertainty and loss of direction. You have to search to find a statesman with an overarching world-view that makes sense. 'There is a void in the main seats of power,' as someone has said, 'the world is on auto-pilot, and no one knows where we are going.'

Faithful people, civil servants and colleagues from the Catholic Centre and the Ecumenical Association have kept tryst with the *lieu de recueillement* over the years, seeking the possibilities that Dag Hammarskjöld was filled with—beyond the frontiers of politics, economics or diplomacy. Yet since his death in a mysterious plane crash in the Congo in September 1961, the life-style of officials of international institutions like the UN or the EU, rather than becoming more measured and reflective, has become a frantic race against time. The vision and purpose that inspired politicians and civil servants in the early years of the European Communities are rare today. Making time to collect one's thoughts in peace is more necessary than ever. Perhaps the *lieu de recueillement* is more organised than Hammarskjöld would have liked, a bit too religious. But besides the services and weekly prayers, regular meetings are held to stimulate thinking and discussion outwith the institutional agenda.

At one such meeting in the *lieu de recueillement*, a French anthropologist, Patrick Viveret, raised 'the question of spirituality', which he described as 'the relationship between democracy and the art of living.' 'One of the determining factors,' he said, 'dealing with all the changes that concern us rests on the quality of *serenity* of groups and individuals, in particular the radical distinction to be maintained between urgency and over-hastiness. They are often confused nowadays. As everything is becoming more urgent no prioritising is possible and the deciders themselves live in anxiety, dealing with this anxiety in haste. Our society needs the exact opposite. It needs to construct spaces of calm and wisdom, in order to be able to deal better with truly urgent questions when they arise. Knowing how to live and learning how to die is becoming a political question.'[3]

---

[3] Patrick Viveret, 'Anthropological Considerations for a Changing World', in *Critical Reflections on the Culture of the West*, ed. Alastair Hulbert, Occasional Paper No. 1, AOES, Brussels, 1995, p. 44.

In an entry in *Markings* dated simply 25.12.55, Dag Hammarskjöld imagined himself going beyond the known: 'In a dream I walked with God through the deep places of creation; past walls that receded and gates that opened, through hall after hall of silence, darkness and refreshment—the dwelling-place of souls acquainted with light and warmth—until, around me, was an infinity into which we all flowed together and lived anew, like the rings made by raindrops falling upon wide expanses of calm dark waters.'[4]

---

[4] Hammarskjöld, *op. cit.*, p. 105.

The language of Yes

O récompense après une pensée
Qu'un long regard sur le calme des dieux![1]
Paul Valéry, *Le Cimetière Marin*

Alone I sit at the grave side of Paul Valéry, shading my eyes against the brilliant light of the October day and the shimmering Mediterranean Sea, contemplating the coastline, the white stone Fort St Pierre and the graveyard by the sea. The place, the past and the poetry lend an elegiac awareness to the present.

These lines from *Le Cimetière Marin* are engraved on Valéry's tombstone. It is by the name of this, his best known poem, that Sète's St Charles Cemetery is commonly known. 'The calm of the gods', the ancient gods of the classical Mediterranean culture Valéry loved, seems to linger here. St Peter's Fort, now the Théâtre Jean Vilar, sits on the corniche below. The grave of Jean Vilar—the great actor and founder of the Avignon Festival and the Théâtre National Populaire—is not far away. The modern troubadour, Georges Brassens, another native of Sète, is buried on the far side of the hill.

Sète is situated at the foot of a wooded hill which rises like a cone above the shoreline of Languedoc. The hill would be an island between the sea and the lagoon but for two sandbanks which attach it to the mainland. These are constantly renewed with sand washed along the coast from the mouth of the Rhône, over fifty miles to the east— tons and tons of pulverized stone from the Alps swept down the great river to the sea.

In an essay entitled *Mediterranean Inspirations*, written as he approached old age, Valéry describes the formative influences of his childhood in Sète. For him the Mediterranean was 'the ever-eventful sea, creator of extraordinary forms and projects, mother of Aphrodite and soul-giver to many an adventure.' Swimming was his great delight, the activity 'nearest to love'. The sea 'has its being in the heart of

---

[1]   Ah what a recompense after a thought
      Gazing long on the calm of the gods!
      The Graveyard by the Sea

poetry,' he wrote, 'Through *her* I am the man I wish to be.' Nor does it change for all its changing forms. The eye sees it exactly as the first man saw it, full of possibilities: *La mer, la mer, toujours recommencée!* 'The mind's contemplation of the sea,' he goes on, 'engenders a vaster desire than any that can be satisfied by the possession of a particular thing.' What he calls the 'pure elements of the moment'—the sky, the sea and the sun—taught him the meaning of infinity, depth, knowledge, the universe: 'the Mediterranean, by reason of its physical features, has played a role or function in the formation of the European mind... A clear sky, a distinct horizon, and an admirable shoreline can not only be the conditions of attracting life and the development of civilisation, but they can stimulate the particular intellectual sensitivity that is scarcely distinct from thought.'[2]

Valéry was writing in the 1930s, at a time when the young Fernand Braudel was formulating his ideas as a historian. With his monumental thesis on the Mediterranean, written from memory in a German prisoner of war camp, Braudel became the great proponent of geographical history, that particularly French approach to historiography which affirms that any reconstruction of the past must include environmental space and involve successive maps and geographies of the place. He shares a vision and a way of looking with the poet Valéry. He meditates on 'the liquid plains of the sea,' the 'creative emptiness' of the Mediterranean, 'the astonishing liberty of its ways through the water.'

'My feeling,' he writes in *The Mediterranean and Mediterranean World in the Age of Philip II,* 'is that the sea itself, the one we see and love, is the greatest document of its past existence... The Mediterranean is not even a single sea, it is a complex of seas; and these seas are broken up by islands, interrupted by peninsulas, ringed by intricate coastlines. Its life is linked to the land, its poetry more than half-rural, its sailors may turn peasant with the seasons; it is the sea of vineyards and olive trees just as much as the sea of the long-oared galleys and the roundships of merchants and its history can no more be separated from that of the lands surrounding it than the clay can be separated from the hands of the potter who shapes it.'[3]

---

[2] *The Collected Works of Paul Valéry*, vol. 15, ed. Jackson Mathieu, Routledge and Kegan Paul, London, 1975, pp. 19-35.

[3] Fernand Braudel, *The Mediterranean and Mediterranean World in the Age of Philip II*, trans. Siân Reynolds, Harper Collins, London, 1992, pp. x, xi.

Transfer such reflections to the Atlantic seaboard of France and the coastline of Brittany half a century later, and you hear echos of Kenneth White speaking in terms of what he calls geopoetics. 'A world is what emerges from the relation between man and the earth. When this relation is sensible, intelligent, complex, the world is world in the deep sense of the word: a beautiful space to live in fully...' Geopoetics 'is founded on the desire of the individual to have a place in the universe in the most dense, the most intense, and at the same time the most liberated, the most "empty" way possible ...'[4]

A sense of place—either from long-term belonging or from having just arrived, it doesn't matter—becomes meaningful as I seek to know and understand it, be accountable to it, make it mine. By appropriating the world in this way, place by place, it becomes part of my culture and identity.

*   *   *

The old town of Sète clusters colourfully round its canals and fishing ports and harbours. The sea is ever present, but there is more to it than just the sea. Mont St Clair rises six hundred feet behind the town to the destination of a cross. Its steep roads are rudimentary thoroughfares between a web of cul-de-sacs. From the graveyard by the sea, the road mounts the Pilgrim's Way, *le Chemin des Pélerins*, past scores of narrow winding ways to nowhere, nerve ends in the body of the island with the feel immemorial of flora and fauna.

Impasse de l'Aurore	of the dawn
Impasse de l'Orée du Bois	of the wood's edge
Impasse du Soleil	of the sun
Impasse des Rêves	of dreams
Impasse des Agaves	of aloes
Impasse du Chèvrefeuille	of the honeysuckle
Impasse du Fenouil	of fennel
Impasse de la Salsepareille	of salsaparilla
Impasse des Tilleuls	of the lime-trees

---

[4] Kenneth White, *Cahiers de Géopoétique* No. 5, Trébeurden, France, 1996, p. 5, my translation.

Impasse des Tamaris	of the tamarisk
Impasse des Aubépines	of hawthorns
Impasse des Lauriers Tins	of laurels
Impasse des Chênes Verts	of the holm oaks
Impasse du Lierre	of ivy
Impasse des Acanthes	of acanthus
Impasse des Oeillets	of pinks
Impasse des Olivettes	of the olive groves
Impasse des Pommettes	of crab-apples
Impasse des Tourterelles	of the turtle-doves
Impasse du Roitelet	of the wren
Impasse du Hérisson	of the hedgehog
Impasse de la Tortue	of the tortoise
Impasse de la Grenouille	of the frog
Impasse des Grillons	of crickets
Impasse des Abeilles	of bees
Impasse du Scarabée	of the beetle
Impasse des Criquets	of the locusts
Impasse de la Fourmi	of the ant
Impasse de la Cigale	of the cicada
Impasse des Lucioles	of fire-flies
Impasse de la Baraquette	of the little boat
Impasse des Chabanettes	of tiny huts
Impasse des Filets	of the nets
Impasse du Nid	of the nest
Impasse de Roche-brune	of the brown rock
Impasse des Rocailles	of the grotto
Impasse des Tonnelles	of the arbours
Impasse de Costebelle	of the lovely coast
Impasse de la Lagun	of the lagoon
Impasse des Embruns	of spindrift
Impasse des Brisants	of the breakers

33

Impasse de l'Écume	of foam
Impasse de l'Ardent	of the ardent one
Impasse des Poètes	of the poets
Impasse des Amourettes	of love-affairs
Impasse d'Oc	of Yes

Sète's delicate affair with Languedoc,
time's intercourse with history:
nature and culture wedded in a place
where the geography is poetry.

Egmond aan Zee
Subject to the wind and the sea

The frailty of life makes Hollanders of us all,
inhabitants each of our own nether lands,
living beneath the level of the waters,
subject to the wind and the sea.

My friend Corien is minister of the Hervormde Kerk in Egmond aan
Zee, an ancient village on the North Sea coast of Holland, not far
from Haarlem. What she said in her sermon that Sunday I didn't
really follow, but the exhilarating reformation hymn we sang, curiously
joyful in its minor mode, was in harmony with the precarious
environment of sand dunes and coarse marram grass, and the scent
of wild thyme.

The simple interior of her church is bright with white-washed
walls and tall clear windows which fill the sanctuary with light. The
paving of the aisle is made of grey slate gravestones from an earlier
church, *mementos mori* of another age. Did the congregation who buried
this English sea captain send to let his loved ones know his ship was
wrecked and he had drowned?

HIER LEYT CAP^T TOMAS
HOUWERT VAN HUL
GESTRANT DEN 20
NOUEMB 1704

There is no cross above the communion table, but high up
beside the ornate canopied pulpit which dominates the sanctuary, framed
by a window, hangs the model of a ship under full sail. As if the boat
were the real symbol of the community that has gathered here, year in
year out, to worship, celebrate and grieve. The boat is a *pinck*, a broad-
beamed, flat-bottomed, Noah's ark-like sailing boat such as fishermen
and sailors used for in-shore fishing or to transport goods along the
coast of Holland where there are few harbours and only sand to beach
ships on. There are no working *pincken* left now though they served
the coastal communities for the best part of four hundred years. The

35

man who made the model still lives in Egmond, but no boat-builder survives. No carpenter for that matter still builds barrel-vaulted ceilings like the one in the church resembling in shape and workmanship a *pinck's* hull upside-down.

The church which was built in 1746 replaced an earlier building. Jacob van Ruisdael's seventeenth century painting of Egmond aan Zee is of a village amongst dunes, its steep roofed houses' gable ends facing streets which converge on an enormous church which dominates the scene. Between 1714 and 1741, the sea claimed the church and half the 250 houses that made up the village. Engravings in the local museum show the square tower balanced over the beach in various stages of collapse, till finally it fell in a pile of rubble. Within one generation! It was a catastrophe for the closed community that Egmond was. Small wonder apocalyptic preachers thrived in Holland, blowing their trumpets against the sins of a people threatened by the aggression of the sea.

Egmond has a 'sea village landscape' like the other coastal villages with no harbour—dunes behind a sea wall of sand with plots of land between them where the sand has been flattened and fertilised and watered for centuries to produce harvests of onions, leeks, potatoes, beans, maize, cabbages, gladioli and sunflowers. Rabbits live there, and foxes are returning after a long absence. Four gull's eggs was the first gift Corien received from a member of her congregation; then came ten hen's eggs from birds reared in the dunes. Corien's husband Thijs keeps bees in a valley called *De Kweek* (the grasslands). The old socialist who gave him his hives stores his socialist books in his hut in the dunes. On a fine day he will sit reading while the bees are at work all around him. We watched from a distance as Thijs and Jara, their six-year old daughter, dressed in masks, coats, gloves and boots, tended their bees.

The dunes are still threatened. Every couple of years a colossal engineering operation, involving ships with huge suction pipes, is deployed to retrieve and replace the sand which is constantly washed away from the fifty miles of beach between Den Haag and Den Helder, leaving the coastline with no protection from tides and storms and the threat of further erosion. The fact that Egmond with its population of 8,000 now takes in well over a million holiday-makers and tourists each year adds vast local, economic pressure to the enterprise. Schemes are discussed to alleviate the erosion by breaching the defence line of high man-made dunes maintained to protect the coast, and letting the sea once again flood certain polders inside.

Walking with Corien and Thijs along the beach one evening to the sounds of the last holiday-makers of the day—bathers, footballers, kite fliers, promenaders—we watched the great orange ball of the sun sink into the sea. Rows of modesty shelters above the high tide mark serve as a reminder of the nineteenth century European bourgeois' discovery of the joys of North Sea bathing. A lighthouse towers over the village, unmanned now, strangely neglected in this technocratic age—as though ships' captains don't need lights and foghorns, for nature has been mastered by a superior technology. Easy enough to believe on a summer evening at the still point between the tide's ebb and flow!

Lat de kust met rust (Leave the coast in peace) is written on posters everywhere in Egmond. It marks the people's opposition to proposals to construct an off-shore island to extend Amsterdam's Schipol Airport. The movement campaigns for 'an undamaged horizon'. Debate is fast and furious as to whether the Dutch government's vast financial surplus from North Sea gas revenue should be spent on the 'hardware' of new infrastructures like an airport, or on 'software' to create the culture, conditions and relationships for a different social contract. Thijs is an ecologist and environmental campaigner. For him it's a matter of participative democracy versus free market technocracy.

What is appropriate technology in Europe? That is the question. And who decides? Must a technique necessarily be employed, just because the means and know-how for it are available? Is efficiency all we have to go for? What about sufficiency? The very questions sound pathetic in view of the quickening pace and lengthening stride of Western technology. The environmental debate in Egmond illustrates well how European civilisation has been both ennobled and estranged by its power and wealth. It is a monopolistic culture that has stubbornly failed to take into account how advances and advantages on the large, technocratic scale necessarily involve compromise and loss on the small-scale, human level; a tragic ideology that would gain the whole world at the cost of losing its soul. The legend of Faust is surely the quintessential myth of modernity!

In Milan Kundera's novel, *Immortality*, there is a searching reflection about the meaning of European civilisation: 'Now, perhaps,

37

when the end of our century provides us with the proper perspective, we can allow ourselves to say: Goethe is a figure placed precisely in the centre of European history. Goethe: the great centre. Not the centre in the sense of a timid point that carefuly avoids extremes, no, a firm centre that holds both extremes in a remarkable balance which Europe will never know again ...'

And, after justifying his point with several examples: 'Goethe lived during that brief span of history when the level of technology already gave life a certain measure of comfort but when an educated person could still understand all the devices he used. Goethe knew how and with what materials his house had been constructed, he knew why his oil lamp gave off light, he knew the principle of the telescope with which he ... looked at Jupiter, and while he himself could not perform surgery, he was present at several operations and when he was sick he could converse with the doctor in the vocabulary of an expert. The world of technical objects was completely open and intelligible to him. This was Goethe's great moment at the centre of European history.'[1]

Such considerations make no impact on the Royal Dutch/ Shell Group's report, *Global Scenarios 1995-2020*, a large-scale assessment of the world ethos after the end of the Cold War. 'Whatever the future holds,' Shell states, 'it will be shaped by three powerful forces: liberalisation, globalisation, and technology. No alternative economic or ideological model competes with the emerging global consensus about the value of open markets and the necessity for macro-economic prudence. This consensus has gathered strength through the globalising influence of technology, especially information technology. What the world has learned in the 1990s is that THERE IS NO ALTERNATIVE to adapting to these powerful forces—TINA.'

The study has two 'scenarios' to illustrate how its one-track future might develop—one Western and one Asian—within the closed circle of which there is no other way to choose. 'Pragmatic ideologies ..., complex adaptive systems ..., enforcing the rules of the game ..., strategies for success ..., competitive advantage ..., an environment of relentless change ..., evolving information technologies ..., bubbles of opportunity ..., bubbles of value ..., a new synthesis ..., history is on

---

[1] Milan Kundera, *Immortality*, trans. Peter Kussi, Faber and Faber, London, 1991, pp. 84-85.

their side ..., integrity is all you've got ..., there is no alternative ...'[2] It is a humourless, Cartesian monopoly that reduces the fullness of life to a barren economicism. Technological civilisation would transform the human condition at the expense of what it means to be human. *Le Monde Diplomatique* calls it *la pensée unique*.

In the 1930s Eugen Rosenstock-Huessy reflected critically on the Russian Revolution: 'Man can live as man only because he can choose various ways of approach to the organisation of mankind. He cannot be limited to one social or economic system. Systems are man-made. In consequence of this truism, man can never be enslaved by his own tools. The whole talk of a one-principle economy seems inhuman ... Any working economy always has been and always will have to be a polyphonic economy ...'[3]

By the late middle ages, the Catholic Church had lost much of its spiritual inspiration and vocation. The Inquisition with its message of *extra ecclesiam, nulla salus* was an effort to compensate. At the end of the age of modernity, as science, technology and economics seem to have shrugged off so much of their enlightened, humanist vocation, a new, more discrete, inquisition is being installed: *liberalisation, globalisation and technology, there is no alternative*. TINA is Shell's gospel for the twenty-first century, the Newspeak of the top transnational corporations. In its pursuit of the better, TINA disregards the good.

There is a mythic dimension to Shell's pronouncements, that would reap a mythic reward. I visited Delphi recently. Delphi may represent no more than the archeology of a European civilisation that is dead and gone, but like a European Macchu Picchu it still puts other cultures into perspective. The magnificent sweep of the site of the sanctuary of Apollo, the scale and colour of the cliffs of Mount Parnassus which rise a thousand feet behind the ruins, the innumerable names of slaves freed after the completion of the temple, engraved on the polygonal wall that still holds up its foundations, the thought that this was the holiest of Greek sanctuaries for well over fifteen hundred years. The very idea of a TINA monopoly on the future would have been absurd and ridiculous to the gods of Olympus. What would have been the response of Apollo or an angry Zeus to the

---

[2] Royal Dutch/Shell Group, *Global Scenarios 1995-2020.*
[3] Eugen Rosenstock-Huessy, *Out of Revolution: Autobiography of Western Man,* Argo Books, Norwich, Vt., 1938 and 1969, p. 732.

hybris of Shell's researchers two millennia later? Look at what happened to Prometheus, or to Atlas.

Global Scenarios 1995-2020 is presented as if Shell believes its own rhetoric, but there is reason to doubt whether such totalitarian thinking is ever accompanied by complete conviction. The wise researchers of Royal Dutch/Shell Group surely know the lie in the argument that there is no alternative. Compare them to Dostoevsky's Grand Inquisitor. For *miracle, mystery and authority* in an age of ecclesiastical hierarchy, read *liberalisation, globalisation and technology* in our age of economic monopoly. The Grand Inquisitor was well aware of the enormity of his rejection of freedom. And he was aware of the consequences too. In Ivan Karamazov's legend of Seville the 'wise old man' speaks to his silent prisoner about the 'terrible and wise spirit, the spirit of self-destruction and non-existence,' whom he serves. 'I tell you,' he says, 'man has no more agonizing anxiety than to find someone to whom he can hand over with all speed the gift of freedom with which the unhappy creature is born. But only he can gain possession of men's freedom who is able to set their conscience at ease ... did you forget that a tranquil mind and even death is dearer to man than free choice in the knowledge of good and evil?'[4]

*   *   *

T'Skai (the separation, in Egmond dialect), divides the Egmond dunes from the Bergen dunes, further up the coast. Egmond's dunes and valleys stretch several miles along the coast and a mile or so inland. All have names, simple names with ancient roots and an echo of geopoetic integrity to resist what 'the spirit of self-destruction and non-existence' is doing in our world.

The land of digging	*De Gravendal*
The field of swans	*Het Zwanenvlak*
The blue grass fields	*'t Zegeveld*
America	*Amerika*
The valley of figs	*De Vijgendal*

---

[4] Dostoevsky, *The Brothers Karamazov*, trans. David Magarshack, Penguin Books, London, 1958, p. 288f.

The valley of berries	*Het Bessiesdal*
The land of stars	*Het Starrenvlak*
The croft	*De Kroft*
The shining place	*De Blink*
The dead valley	*De Dooie Dal*
The dunes of Jan Bakkum	*De Duintjes van Jan Bakkum*
Crown City	*De Kroonstad*
Job de Vrij's valley	*Job de Vrij z'n Dal*
Rabbit valley	*Konijnendal*
The water pits	*De Waterkuilen*
Klaas the Cat's valley	*Klaas de Kat z'n Dal*
Coen van Duin's valley	*Coen van Duin z'n Dal*
Aldert's valley	*Aldert z'n Dal*
Dune of the man of bells	*Bellemansdal*
Where once the ship, where twice	*Eerste Soeckebacker*
the ship Soeckebacker	*'t Tweede Soeckebacker*
(foundered)	

Cluj and Păltinoasa
To keep the landscape on purpose

*The arrow of progress is broken and the future has lost its
brightness: what it holds in store are more threats than promises.*[1]

In the sixties it was theological journals for a seminary in Naumberg
smuggled under my shirt through the Berlin U-Bahn. In the seventies,
a tape recorder and religious books on the roof of our Land Rover
bound for Prague. In the eighties, off to Nicaragua, my rucksack bulging
with a typewriter for a base community and a volley ball net for the
prison in Estelí. Now, in the late nineties, it is a small car laden with two
second-hand computers, a couple of printers and various spare parts
for women's associations working to reconstruct civil society in eastern
Europe.

But NATO bombs were falling on Yugoslavia. They scored a
direct hit on our plans to visit Voyvodina. So Rosa who is from Novi
Sad and Yasmina from the border town of Subotica came to meet us
in Budapest instead. They represented partner organisations and
brought with them beautiful wooden toys and enchanting Croatian
peasant art—pictures and greetings cards made of straw—for us to
sell in Scotland. We had a printer and computer parts for them. We
drove them back to the border, to deliver them once more to the air
raids and the cuts in electricity and water, to the dangers and hardships
of a war they failed to understand and wanted no part in. Which is
how we found ourselves in a seriously overloaded car driving south
from Budapest on the motorway to Szeged.

Yasmina is an ethnic Croat, married to an ethnic Hungarian.
Rosa is a Jew. Though NATO was bombing Voyvodina as if it were
part of Serbia, the region has a great mix of peoples and cultures, the
legacy of the Austro-Hungarian Empire. The fault line which divides
Eastern Orthodoxy and Islam from Western Christianity follows the
marches of the former empire, east of Transylvania, south of
Voyvodina, through Sarajevo and Mostar to the sea. On both sides
the mix is potent, as the conflicts and atrocities of the 1990s have

---

[1] Wolfgang Sachs, *The Development Dictionary*, Zed Books, London, 1992, p. 2.

revealed. The beautiful arched bridge over the River Neretva at Mostar, built in 1566 (*most* means bridge in Serbo-Croat), a symbol of exchange across that great divide, was finally destroyed by Serb and Croat shelling on 13th November 1993.

After an ice cream in the old town square of Szeged and bidding farewell to our friends from the other side, my wife and I set out in the early afternoon for Transylvania. The journey took ten hours. Having braved the hazards of night driving in Romania, we arrived in Cluj.

*   *   *

Our ethnic Hungarian friends, Korši and Ildiko, are intellectuals and the walls of their sitting room were stacked high with books. Conversation about the war led to the question whether the ethnic mix of Transylvania could spill over into another conflict there. Korši was a historian and he hadn't much confidence in Romanian democracy, but he didn't think so. The roots of cohabitation and cooperation were too old and deep. To Europeans, the Magyars were barbarians who came from the foothills of the Ural Mountains, eventually invading the Middle Danube Basin eleven hundred years ago. Hungary was brought into the fold of Western civilisation a century later when, in 1001, the Pope crowned Stephen I, King and Apostle. Stephen's policies of a millennium ago, favouring a certain form of interculturalism, are worth studying today. In his beautiful long hand Korši copied out for me the Latin text of one of ten precepts on good governance which St Stephen wrote for his son a thousand years ago. It goes like this:

> Such great advantage comes from foreigners and immigrants that they well deserve their position as the sixth element of royal dignity. For that is how the Roman empire first arose, and the kings of Rome became exalted and famous, because many celebrated and wise men flocked there from different places. In fact Rome would be in chains until today, if the sons of Aeneas had not made it free. For as foreigners come from different places and regions, so they bring with them different languages and customs, and different lessons and tools, which adorn all estates and extol princely power and frighten away

the arrogance of outward things. Thus government by a single language and with a single code of conduct is weak and frail.

Therefore I bid you, my son, foster them with a good will and defend them honourably, so that they choose you willingly wherever they live. For if you destroy what I have built up, or seek to disperse what I have united, your royal government will undoubtedly be exposed to the greatest detriment. If this is not so, your government will increase daily, so that your crown will be held in esteem by men.[2]

*   *   *

Laura is the wife of Radu, the Orthodox priest in Păltinoasa, a village near Gura Humorului in Bucovina, north-eastern Romania. She is a warm and generous person, the mother of three young children. Their village lies over the Carpathian Mountains, in foothills which begin to have the feel of the plains of Moldavia. We were their guests. We drove there in an afternoon from the old town centre of Tîrgu Mures, gradually leaving behind the industrial and economic wasteland that surrounds the city, the disheartening signs of Caucescu's domination, climbing out of Transylvania through spas and meadow land into the forests which cover the rolling hills.

The changing features of village architecture along the roadside are like the transformation in the shape and taste of bread, from nan to pitta, that I observed on a journey overland from Peshawar to Jerusalem many years ago. The vernacular forms and elements of cultures reflect living conditions and particular choices which vary from place to place. There are low, painted cottages in the foothills, their wide vine-covered eves making for shady verandahs which run the full length of the house. The timber buildings in the mountains are as sturdy as north American log cabins, though the wood is typically square dressed and covered with lath and plaster. The orientation of the village houses varies along the way, parallel to the road or at right angles to it. So many houses now are in the process of improvement

---

[2] Stephen I, *Brief Concerning the Institution of Customs: On Receiving and Fostering Foreigners*, my translation.

and extension. But there are also incongruous, nouveau riche extravaganzas, as often as not unfinished and unlived in—a blight on the beautiful countryside, and as tasteless as a pan loaf in Isfahan.

The priest's house in Păltinoasa is a solid four-square building in the Hungarian style, a reminder of the fact that Bucovina was annexed by the Hapsburgs in 1785. Its spacious verandah, central hall and five large rooms allow ample space for guests. In the yard outside there are ducks and hens, goats and a pig, as well as a couple of dogs and a cat. The covered well remains the source of water for the home though an electric pump now maintains the supply. Beside the yard is an orchard full of apple trees in blossom, which partially hide the view of the stork's nest on the nearby telegraph pole. Well before dawn, still half-asleep, I hear the clip-clop, clip-clop of horses on the road, taking peasants in their carts to work.

The twelve Orthodox monasteries of Bucovina, set in their mediaeval compounds, have recently been returned, with UNESCO's help, to the glory of their early years. Several of them have monastic communities once more, as nuns have taken up a lifestyle interrupted over two hundred years ago. The outside walls of the monastery churches are famous for their frescoes, rich and lavish in both colour and imagery. The paintings have survived remarkably well, except on the northern sides where centuries of rain have washed much of the polychrome away. The mediaeval artists' colours vie with the Renaissance, the deep red of Humor, Voronet blue, the yellow of Moldovita, emerald green of Susevita. The art critic, André Lwoff, speaks of the 'heroism' of the painting with which the painters dared nature 'to keep the landscape on purpose, in order to ensure an ambience fit for man's accomplishment.' At Voronet the sheltered western wall carries a huge fresco in five storeys of the Last Judgement, an Eastern Orthodox equivalent of Michelangelo's Last Judgement in the Sistine Chapel.

Over a glass of plumb brandy after dinner with Radu and Laura and some of their friends, another priest told the story of a conversation he once had when working as a guide in the monasteries. He was showing a group of French tourists around when in the midst of a conversation about church architecture one of the Frenchmen said rather condescendingly, 'The Bucovina monasteries are very beautiful, but they're nothing compared to the Cathedral of Notre Dame.' To which the young priest replied, 'Monsieur, if it were not

45

for the monasteries of Bucovina and their defence of Europe, there would be no Notre Dame de Paris!'

Both Hungarians and Romanians in modern Romania claim the credit for protecting Christendom from successive attacks from the east. In the twelfth and thirteenth centuries the Hungarians invited a mix of German settlers into Transylvania, knights, burghers, artisans and miners, to rebuild a landscape which had been destroyed by the Mongol invasions and defend it against further threats. They were allowed extensive cultural autonomy and self-government. Only now are the last of the Germans in the Sieben Burgen, the Seven Fortress Towns they built, being 'repatriated' to the Federal Republic, like diaspora Jews to modern Israel.

The 'monastic archipelago' in the north-east corner of Romania is also associated with the defence of Europe against Turks and Tartars. The Siege of Constantinople is a common subject of the frescos on the monastery walls. After Constantinople fell to the Turks in 1453, it seemed as if Islam would sweep across this western promontory of Asia. Putna, the oldest monastery, was founded in the 1460s by another St Stephen, King Stephen the Great, who was surnamed 'Athlete of Christ' for his part in defending Europe. He claimed to have fought thirty-six battles in his lifetime, of which he won thirty-four. It is said that he built a church and fathered a son after each of his victories! So the monastery churches are a tangible symbol of the defence of Europe.

Neal Ascherson, in his book, *Black Sea,* expresses a healthy doubt about the continuing idea that the people from the steppes present a threat to Europe. It was, he argues, nineteenth century 'pseudo-anthropology' which fed 'the basic European nightmare: a terror of peoples who move. This nightmare, inherited from the great migrations during and after the decline of the Roman Empire and renewed by the Hun and Mongol raids into the West, was given an extra dimension of horror by nineteenth-century evolutionist intellectuals ... That nightmare survives in the new Europe after the revolutions of 1989. It survives as Western fear of all travelling people ...'[3]

The iconography of the monasteries' exterior walls has been described as 'an open book with a biblical content'. One fresco that

---

[3] Neal Ascherson, *Black Sea: the Birthplace of Civilisation and Barbarism*, Vintage, London, 1996, p. 76.

has survived on the north wall of Voronet depicts Adam ploughing—
a scene surprisingly common in the reality of Moldova today, with no
difference in technique from ancient times or from the fifteenth or
sixteenth centuries when the fresco was painted—a peasant with oxen
or horses ploughing a single furrow. Misha, a friend from Bucharest
who accompanied us on our travels, lamented the lost opportunities in
land reform following the Caucescu era. The technical equipment that
remained was for the most part squandered and there is now no capital
to buy more. The result is a primitive agricultural industry with no
diversity. Orchards are untended and, except for meadows and some
strip farming, much of the land lies uncultivated. However, the
challenge to find a balance between labour-intensive and technology-
intensive agriculture is still there. The investment required to develop
a more self-reliant system would not need to be as crippling as under
even a revised EU Common Agricultural Policy.

Laura, who is a part-time teacher (though she has not been
paid for two months), is an optimist. 'Everything is natural here,' she
says, indicating the bright yoke yellow of her home baking, 'Fresh
eggs and milk for the children—I know exactly which hens and cows
they're from. There's the apple orchard, the animals and poultry in the
yard—and,' she laughs, 'the storks.'

She was very pleased with the computer we brought for the
new village association she runs. Its name translates, 'Women are Strong'.
'We had no social life for fifty years,' she says, thinking of the joys and
tribulations of grassroots organising. She is sociable and increasingly
fulfilled in that domain. Yet she remains content with the tiled wood
stove built into the central stem of her house, the appliances in her
kitchen and bathroom, the local produce and village life. Her sense of
well-being is not subject to talk of development. She doesn't think in
terms of commodities that must be bought. The traditional Orthodox
spirituality of her way of life, her *orthopraxis*, has a well-tried capacity
for self-reliance and survival. The materialism and consumerism of
the West are still at bay. Her common sense carries an awareness of
limits. Needs and rights are concepts as yet alien to her culture.

Under Caucescu's regime Bucovina was to a great extent by-
passed by 'development'. And for the time being Romania as a whole,
let alone its far north-east, hardly qualifies in the world league for
development. In today's economic dispensation, as defined by the World
Bank and the European Union, this might well be a privilege. Laura's

optimism reminded me of what the Mexican Gustavo Esteva used to say in the 1980s about the peasants in Mexico City.

He welcomed the crisis that hit Mexico in the early 1980s when it couldn't pay its international debt due to falling oil prices, the collapse in the living standards of the middle class, political corruption and environmental degradation. The contradictions inherent in economic 'certainties' became more and more apparent. Fortunately, according to Esteva, the crisis happened in time, before the culture of self-reliance of millions of peasants who had migrated from the countryside to the city in the 1970s had been completely outmoded and forgotten. There was still a possibility that the conception of personal well-being and the common weal might be delinked from 'development', and alternatives, based on old wisdom and practice, rediscovered. To be by-passed by development would eventually be seen to be an advantage.

> Development means to have started on a road that others know better, to be on your way towards a goal that others have reached, to race up a one-way street. Development means the sacrifice of environments, solidarities, traditional interpretations and customs to ever changing expert advice. Development promises enrichment, and for the overwhelming majority, has always meant the progressive modernisation of their poverty: growing dependence on guidance and management.[4]

I hope Radu and Laura and their children will not have to suffer development. I hope Bucovina—a rich and beautiful land, poor as it has always been, yet not impoverished and humiliated like other regions of Romania—might have the heroism to keep the landscape on purpose. Who knows, that might have something in it of a new defence of Europe!

---

[4] Gustavo Esteva, 'Development: Metaphor, Myth, Threat', in *Development: Seeds of Change*, 1985: 3, SID, Rome.

The backs of Brussels

Un jour pourtant un jour viendra couleur d'orange
Un jour de palme un jour de feuillages au front
Un jour d'épaule nue où les gens s'aimeront
Un jour comme un oiseau sur la plus haute branche[1]
Aragon, *Le fou d'Elsa*

First day of summer, and the dawn chorus woke me—like an echo from afar, like a piano's muffled playing in the house next door— tentative at first but gaining clarity and strength: rising, falling, overflowing, drawing me out of the depths of sleep.

The backs which our bedroom overlooks are lush with the growth from recent rains. The moist earth is fragrant. Last night the air in the attic room was hot and stifling. Its coolness now comes from the large windows which were open all night long. The boulevard on the far side of the house is still. Four something in the morning, and first one, then another birdsong preludes a growing clamour of birds, each singing its heart out, reaffirming its place in the world. The blackbird leads, next the thrush, then chaffinches, blue tits and great tits, more and more, with pigeons cooing in the background. Artless counterpoint! Never was nature's instinct for life more convincing. And most other *Bruxellois* are still asleep, oblivious to the new day's dawning.

City life in Brussels can be very pleasant. The three and four-storey terraced houses lining the streets in the older neighbourhoods are typically all different from each other. The Horta museum in St Gilles, the house and workshop which the architect Victor Horta built for himself a century ago, is an exceptional monument to Art Nouveau. But not so unique that his influence can't be recognised in the delicate

---

[1] One day, but yes, a day will come the colour of orange
A day of waving palms a day crowned with wreathes
A day to slip out of things where folk will be in love
A day like a bird on the topmost branch
(My translation)

facades, the glass and ironwork, the curves and inverse curves of countless early 20th century houses around town. And tucked away behind the houses are secluded gardens, havens of green peace, the *alter ego* of the cosmopolitan culture of Europe's capital.

Our home is a converted attic flat on a busy thoroughfare, but with most of its windows at the back. The high, spacious, balcony with its wooden decking gets what sun there is all day, all year round. By June the geraniums in their pots and window boxes burn like fire against the background of the cluttered tiles and worn brick walls of the surrounding houses. A dozen or more long narrow gardens, divided at sixes and sevens by walls topped with glazed tiles, fill the large square behind.

Each garden is a world unto itself. From our vantage point we profit from them all. In summer, the trees and bushes, lawns and flowers offer a comfortable location for the neighbours' lazy conversations, barbeques and children's games, for cavorting dogs and stalking cats. *C'est gai!* as they say in Brussels. Once we heard sheep, and made out through thick leaves some gardens down a couple of fat lambs cropping the grass. To sit on the balcony in the evening, watching the sun go down behind the trees, behind the distant towers and tower blocks of the city skyline, is to put life on hold—to have time to reflect, to remember and connect, simply to be. At sunset the numerous, ominous, vapour trails of aeroplanes criss-crossing the skies are nevertheless rose tinted.

High in the summer sky lives the incomparable swift, fond Nature's Ariel, with its long dark scythe-like wings and high-pitched, muted whistle-scream. It lays its eggs in holes in the roofs and walls of nearby buildings, in the repaired nests of starlings. The foodballs it feeds its young can include as many as a thousand flying insects. When the fledglings leave the nest they face a flight to the farthest tip of southern Africa, where they may spend several years before returning to nest in Europe. They live, feed, drink, sleep, eventually mate, entirely on the wing. The grief of autumn's coming is most sharply felt in the loss of these matchless spirits of the air.

Next door is an ancient cedar tree, its broad, flat, dark green boughs providing shelter and protection for birds of many kinds. When we moved into our flat a flock of collared doves was in permanent residence. Timid creatures with their soft grey-brown plumage and distinctive black collars, they are the Asian ornithological immigrants of the 1950s. Spring inspires them to feats of diving, an instinctive exultation at the seasons turning. Wings flapping passionately, they labour up to an invisible summit in the air. Up, up and over, and with a last quick beat, it's gliding all the way down—to begin again. After rain, they bathe in the puddles of a flat roof. Like the sound of running water or a sleeping baby's breathing, their cooing echoes the rhythm of the earth. They're quite unlike the street pigeons which eventually chased them off and colonised the cedar.

One summer day when our kitchen windows were open wide, a homing pigeon landed on the windowsill. Her grey-blue plumage was like the other pigeons', but she was slimmer, sleeker—and more intelligent too. After a moment to size up the situation, she came on in and made herself at home. I forget what loving things I said to her. With a pert eye she kept me under observation, staying just out of reach of my caresses. She promenaded on the kitchen table for a while, strutting boldly across a plate or two, helping herself to crumbs. The tablecloth was laid out just for her. A ring on her leg bore the number Belg-97 5049066, but I called her Felicity.

For a long time there may be no sign of seagulls. Then, one evening, there they are again. In twos or threes, maybe half a dozen, flying steadily, gracefully, high above the backs. Northwards at evening, southwards in the morning. I've never heard them cry—they aren't like the gulls over Edinburgh, forever crying. Gulls have their own geography and history. Where they come from, I don't know. Where they're going, I don't know. *Dasein:* they're there! Through the window of a lighted room, I watch them fly across the pale reflection of my face, their presence in the evening sky thrown against my existence, my being there.

*   *   *

Jan Van Eyck's painting of the *Madonna with Canon van der Paele* in the Groeninge Museum in Bruges was completed in 1436. It is one of the masterpieces of the Flemish Primitives. The Madonna is seated in the midst of a splendid ecclesiastical decor of tall gothic windows, with houses and lawns outside. To the left is Canon van der Paele, warts and all; on the right St George in armour. The architecture, furnishings and clothing are sumptuous in every detail. The Christ child is seated on his mother's lap, holding a bird. But it's not the usual finch. It's a small green parrot.

51

Philip the Good, Duke of Burgundy (1396-1467), ruler of Flanders, met his fiancée Isabella of Portugal for the first time in Bruges in 1429, but not before he had taken precautions to discover what she looked like! When it was suggested that he take her to be his third wife, he sent Jan Van Eyck to Portugal to paint her portrait. He painted not only Isabella but also the native parrots of the country. Their cry transliterated 'ave'. And *Ave* and its inverse, Eva, were reason enough in Van Eyck's Mariology to paint a parrot in Jesus' hand.

Today Van Eyck wouldn't need to go to Portugal to find his model parrot. There are parrots enough in Brussels, though their shrill cries don't sound quite so pious. The first time I caught sight of one, its brilliant light green plumage was a huge surprise against the dark green foliage of our neighbour's cedar. Later one perched in full view on the next-door garden's birch tree top, the sunlight emblazoning its feathers. Now the flocks of parrots flying overhead are on the increase. They are moving in from the Forêt de Soigne, the great beech forest, south-east of the city. They remind me of the Nicaraguan perroquetes, that live in holes in the crater walls of the Santiago volcano near Masaya, seemingly thriving on the sulphur that rises from the smoking crater. Thin, long-tailed beauties they are, swift as arrows.

The radio reports an illegal trade in exotic birds to the European Union. One hundred parrots smuggled from Zaire to Belgium, half of them dead on arrival.

Were the rest set free?

My friend Michel is the commanding officer in Somoto,
    up by the border with Honduras,
and he told me that he discovered a consignment
        of parrots
which were to be smuggled to the U.S.
    so that there they'd learn to speak English.
There were 186 parrots, and 47 had already died in their
        cages.
And he sent them back to the place they'd been
      taken from,
and when the truck was approaching a place they call
      Los Llanos
close to the mountains those parrots came from
    (the mountains seemed huge behind those plains)

the parrots began to get excited and flap their wings
        and to press themselves against their cage walls.
And when the cages were opened
they all flew off like arrows in the same direction to
        their mountains.
The Revolution did the same thing for us, I'm thinking:
it freed us from the cages in which they were carting us
        off to speak English.
It handed us back the country they'd snatched from us.
Parrot-green compañeros gave the parrots their green
        mountains.
        But there were 47 that died.[2]

*   *   *

How quick you have to be to catch a glimpse of the birds in the backs. Only the heron is slow, 'winnowing the warm air on wide quiet wings' (John Muir). You see it flying from the horizon, far away against the sky, not knowing what it is at first. 'What is the slow, wide-winged figure in the sky?' asks a wistful character in Ursula Le Guin's *Searoad*, '... like a word in a foreign language, like seeing one's own name written in a strange alphabet ...'[3]

The grey heron has adapted well to urban conditions in Europe. On our side of Brussels there are many lakes and ponds in the forests, parks and gardens. Herons regularly cross the city from one stretch of water to another in search of fishing grounds. Yet I've seen one standing on the topmost branch of the silver birch, swaying gently, far from the lure of water, its loneliness etched on the sky. What mournful thoughts pass through its mind?

        Spring is passing by!
        Birds are weeping and the eyes
        Of fish fill with tears[4]

---

[2] Ernesto Cardenal, *Cosmic Canticle,* Canto 18: *Flights of Victory,* trans. John Lyons, Curbstone Press, Willimantic, 1993, pp.171-172.

[3] Ursula Le Guin, *Searoad, Chronicles of Klatsand,* Harper Collins, New York, 1991, p. 157.

[4] Matsuo Bashō, *The Narrow Road to Oku,* trans. Donald Keene, Kodansha International, London, 1996, p. 23.

The heron's flight can be quite disrupted by the angry, energetic intervention of a crow. It is by the crow's attacks on trespassing herons, that you can tell how far crow territory extends across the backs. The crow only persists to a certain point, the limits of its air space. After that it wheels away and returns to its own domain—with obvious self-satisfaction, strutting and preening itself in an effort to regain composure.

A crow couple lives behind our house. Of all the birds theirs is the most powerful presence. Their force of character dominates the backs. They oversee the gardens from the original crow's nests, their look-out points. When one crow calls to another from a house top, its hoarse caw wracks its whole body.

It's not surprising that crows were associated with oracles in ancient times. A glazed pottery drinking vessel from the temple at Delphi—an elegant shallow bowl on a broad stem—depicts the god Apollo with his lyre, sitting on a regal stool, pouring a libation, face to face with a crow. Coronis—related to Chronos, the god of time and death—means crow, and this mysterious bird is and is not the mortal princess Coronis, Apollo's lover. She was with child by him when he left her in Thessaly, guarded by a crow with snow-white feathers, to visit his shrine at Delphi. But during his absence she invited another lover, Ischys, to her couch. The guardian crow, flustered at her infidelity, set out for Delphi to report, but the god had divined Coronis's unfaithfulness already. He cursed the crow for not pecking out Ischys's eyes. The crow turned black, and ever since crows bear the colour of Apollo's curse.[5]

One winter morning there they are, our crows, side by side on the bough of a leafless ash tree, pecking grubs from each other's necks. Front feathers, back and sides, as each bends and stretches to accommodate. By summer there are four of them, the parent birds and two young ones, full grown yet distinguishable by their unkempt style.

The young must learn the crow's philosophy—fend for yourself, be vigilant over your territory, caw with all the conviction of the oracle's injunction to 'know thyself'. At evening when the crow's enigmatic croaking falls silent, the stillness of the backs is palpable.

---

[5] Robert Graves, *The Greek Myths*, Penguin Books, London, 1955, Vol. 1, p. 174.

Tucked away in the dark poetry of Ted Hughes' *Crow* is this luminous interpellation:

> ... what spoke that strange silence
> After his clamour of caws faded?[6]
>
> *(Crow's Theology)*

---

[6] Ted Hughes, *Crow*, Faber and Faber, London, 1972, p. 27.

The stasis of Europe

Oh ! Paris est la cité mère !
Paris est le lieu solennel
Où le tourbillon éphémère
Tourne sur un centre éternel !
Paris ! feu sombre ou pure étoile
Morne Isis couverte d'un voile !
Araignée à l'immense toile
Où se prennent les nations !
Fontaine d'urnes obsédée
Mamelle sans cesse inondée
Où pour se nourrir de l'idée
Viennent les générations ![1]

Victor Hugo, À l'Arc de Triomphe

'C'est par là, monsieur, c'est par là!' It was a young North African, who saw me studying the street map at the exit of the Stalingrad métro station, calling to me though the grill. Stalingrad is on the Northern line, Étoile to Nation. At this stage it runs overground, one great long viaduct sweeping down the middle of the Boulevard de la Chapelle—Barbès-Rochechouart, La Chapelle, Stalingrad, Juarès ... The history of France is in the names of the stations of the Métropolitain! From Sunday market to American-style basketball court, you find it

---

[1] Oh! Paris is the mother city!
  Paris is the solemn spot
  Where the passing whirlwind
  Turns on an eternal centre!
  Paris! dark fire or pure star
  Mournful Isis covered with a veil!
  A spider with its vast web
  In which are caught the nations!
  Fountains whither crowds of people flock
  Breast filled with milk for all to share
  Where generations come
  To drink ideas at its spring!
  (My translation)

under the *aérien:* the street as a way of fife. This is the 19th Arrondissement, next door to the famous Goutte d'Or—high rise social housing full of second and third generation immigrants from Algeria, Tunisia, Morocco, whose parents and grandparents helped establish the prosperity of the European Community. Beyond Stalingrad is the Bassin de la Villette—the great nineteenth century canal port, abandoned now except by tourists in their *bateaux mouches*—and the stately Rotonde de la Villette, the former customs building, facing the broad stretch of waterway where the canal ends.

It was indeed 'par là': Tangiers Street, where the second mosque in Paris houses one of the most vibrant Muslim centres in Europe. The obliging young man had noticed me in the métro, studying a leaflet about the conference I was going to, 'The Mosque in the City'. He was going too, so he showed me the way. Above the entrance to the centre, in big letters, *Que Dieu vous couvre de sa miséricorde.* May God shelter you with his loving kindness.

The *Centre Socio-Culturel de la Rue de Tanger* is housed in a converted three storey warehouse, next door to an imposing municipal primary school, dated 1876. The tower blocks across the narrow street have only a show of grass and trees around them, though the noise of the sparrows there is louder than the traffic. Given that only three months previously a bomb had exploded in front of the mosque, and no one had yet decided whether it was Islamic fundamentalists or French nationalists who did it, it was remarkable, though typical, that the only police presence in the vicinity was of two gendarmes temporarily supervising children crossing the road to the primary school.

A welcoming bustle greeted us at the entrance. Inside, rooms were being prepared and food laid out. The *Mission Populaire* I knew in Paris in the seventies, was like this—a workers' mission founded by a Scot after the Paris Commune. In the 'Miss Pop' however, we were Christians doing things for others: social work, worship and pastoral care for workers, migrants, homeless, women and children. Here it was people from a similar social milieu, but they were Muslims, and doing something for themselves—seeking to establish Islam as a main-stream social and intellectual current in French and European society today.

'C'est moi qui vous ai parlé au téléphone; enchantée de vous connaître!' It was the young woman at the door who had made the arrangements for my visit. She gave me my name badge with a broad smile. Her oval face was framed with a white silk headscarf. About half of the women, who altogether made up about a third of the 250 participants, were wearing headscarves. There were several women organisers too, chairing the sessions. The conference was the final meeting of a series, the culmination of a year's monthly seminars on different aspects of Muslim involvement in society. What with over thirty speakers invited for the panel presentations—French, North African, and others like myself—there was little time for discussion. At least the Muslim community's integration into French rationalism seemed to me a fait accompli! Nevertheless the large audience, predominantly young, was eager and attentive.

A former French senator began his speech with a self-deprecating 'Je ne suis pas intellectuel, ni philosophe, ni poète; je suis un simple fils de paysan.' It was beautiful: the son of an Algerian peasant he may have been—but in his lifetime he had learned philosophy, and if not poetry, at least something of the ancient art of rhetoric. His manner of speaking French was typical of Arabs who are bilingual with French or English—full of surprises, figures of speech and imaginative metaphors, a delight to listen to. At lunch I sat with an old friend. There was couscous with great chunks of tender lamb and a spicy soup of vegetables.

The themes of the conference were remarkably like some Church and Society agendas: the crisis of the French Republic, where inequality is a fact of life; how to promote unity and diversity in French culture, now that the inclusive exclusion of the 'our ancestors, the Gauls' approach of colonial times is over and done with; secular law, in France and the European Union, as the primary means of achieving justice.

It was in 1952 that Alfred Sauvy, the French demographer, coined the term 'Third World', describing Algeria and countries like it as 'this *Third World* which is ignored, exploited, despised like the Third Estate, and also aspires to be something.' That state of affairs has now come home to the metropolis. The 'immigrants' of only a few years ago are called 'Muslims' now, but the change in identification offers little social or cultural improvement. Islam has always been treated as an exception in France, while in Europe as a whole an open debate about the Muslim presence is held hostage by international events and the media fascination with fundamentalism and extremism. How to be free of this? The opening speech of Larbi Kechat, the Rector of the Mosque, was a impassioned appeal for liberation.

*   *   *

Stalingrad is only four short stops from Pigalle, which is one of the underground stations still graced by an art nouveau cast iron gateway. A stone's throw from Place Pigalle—the red light district begins on the other side—there's another archway, wide enough for a carriage to pass. It leads through the terraced buildings of the boulevard into a courtyard with cobblestones, trees and a little garden where children play. Behind it stands a four storey tenement of artists' studios, built in a 19th century style that has all but disappeared. Degas rented a studio here. For a few years in the early 1900s, Picasso had one on the top floor.

Our friends, Didier and Annie, live in Picasso's studio which they have transformed into a delightful apartment. Like many Parisians, they left Paris proper for the *banlieu* when their children were young, but now they're back. The large studio window looks north over half a mile of jumbled, unmistakably Parisian, leaded rooftops as they rise gently to Montmartre Hill, topped by the Basilica of the Sacré Coeur. The view is spectacular. And to think that the Sacré Coeur, this brilliant, exotic symbol of the church triumphant, was built in France *after* the Revolution, to praise God for the successful and bloody repression of the Commune! Paris offers an abundance of such contradictions.

Didier and Annie took us to the Institut du Monde Arabe, an impressive modern monument to Arabism, with theatre and lecture halls, exhibition centre, archive, bookshop and offices, built in the Mitterand years on the left bank of the Seine. The Île St Louis, seen from its rooftop terrace, is exquisite. The French are at their best when it comes to such extravagant manifestations of civilisation, of intellectual solidarity with peoples and cultures they may have ruthlessly exploited for centuries. It's their demonstration (the same but different from our English version) of a certain European naivety—the self-expression of a world power which has insufficient self-awareness to recognise its arrogance and cynicism for what it is. 'With us,' wrote Jean-Paul Sartre in his preface to Fanon's *The Wretched of the Earth,* 'there is nothing more consistent than a racist humanism since the European has only been able to become a man through creating slaves and monsters.'[2] And Franz Fanon himself, in the conclusion of his

---

[2] Frantz Fanon, *The Wretched of the Earth*, Penguin Books, London, 1965, p. 22.

book, calls this self-confident complacency 'the stasis of Europe ... this motionless movement where gradually dialectic is changing into the logic of equilibrium'.[3] What Fanon wrote in 1961 was a foretaste of now, after the end of the Cold War, with the spread of a globalised logic of equilibrium, *la pensée unique*.

*   *   *

If you look out of Didier and Annie's bedroom window, you can just see in the distance across the Seine the Musée d'Orsay. It is a magnificent conversion of a nineteenth century railway station into another cathedral of culture. The collection of French painting it houses is stunning. On the esplanade in front of the entrance, are six larger-than-life bronze statues of seated figures, dating from 1878. They were commissioned for the terrace of the Paris World Exhibition. The sculptors were all different—Alexandre Schonewerk, Alexandre Falguière, Eugène Delaplanche, Ernest Hiolle, Aimé Millet and Maturin Moreau—yet there is a remarkable homogeneity of conception and execution in the works themselves. Anyone who knows the beautiful ornate figures on the ancient world maps engraved in Antwerp or Amsterdam will recognise the connection. These sculptures represent the continents of the world in order of their 'civilisation'—Europe, Asia, Africa, North America, South America and the Pacific (*Océanie*). They are all the more interesting for having been produced in the decade following France's defeat by Prussia in 1871, when an intense public debate was going on about colonisation. Should France follow other European powers and launch into the conquest of a colonial empire, or not?

Europe is dressed in a cloak and armour, with a helmet like Pericles', a breastplate, shield, leather greaves and sandals. In her right hand is an olive branch and in her left a fashioner's hammer. At her side are paint brushes, books and the snake-entwined staff of the physician.

Asia too is fully clothed, but that her bodice falls away to reveal the nipple of one breast. Her head is bare but there are sandals on her feet. Her back is guarded by two elephants and on her lap sits a five-figured idol.

Africa's big right breast is bare. Her left leg is uncovered to the thigh, the bare foot resting on a turtle's back. She holds a wide basket of

---

[3] *Op. cit.* p. 253.

fruit against her hip. A headdress of cloth tops her negroid face, large rings in her ears. Two daggers are tucked into her cummerbund. The seat she sits on is decorated with a bird and beast bas-relief.

North America is a native woman with feathered head-dress and skirt. The cloak over her back is held in place by a necklace of animals' teeth. Her breasts are naked and her feet bare. She wears a band on her wrist and on the ceremonial axe in her hand are inscribed the names of Washington, Lafayette, Franklin and Jefferson.

South America is likewise bare-breasted and bare-footed. She sits on a pile of rocks, to the left of which is a crouching condor. Her simple head-dress is held in place by a thick hairpin. From underneath her long skirt comes a gush of fruit—pineapples, bananas, dates and pomegranates—on which her foot rests. In her right hand is an ornamental shield with the names of countries: Brazil, Peru, Ecuador, Chile, Bolivia, Columbia, Uruguay, Venezuela, Paraguay, Centro America and Rep. Argentina.

Océanie's long hair is held up by a band of rope. The great furskin tied round her shoulders is all she wears. She has large, pointed breasts. By her right hand is a kangaroo, and in her left a club and a barbed knife.

If culture, as Thierry Verhelst reminds us, is 'the sum total of the original solutions that a group of human beings invent to adapt to their natural and social environment',[4] then Europe as represented here is in a class of her own. In addition to her elaborate armour, she has books, tools and symbols well in excess of what the others have. Apart from an idol or two, their dress and weapons, and some names, mostly of European origin—nature rather than culture is supposed to define who they are.

And then there's the fact that they are women, and the state of their undress. Thirty years ago John Berger wrote about the nude in European painting: 'According to usage and conventions … the social presence of a woman is different in kind from that of a man … Men survey women before treating them. Consequently how a woman appears to a man can determine how she will be treated … To be naked is to be oneself. To be nude is to be seen naked by others and yet not recognised for oneself … Women are there to feed an appetite,

---

[4] Thierry Verhelst, *No Life without Roots,* trans. Bob Cumming, Zed Books, London, 1990, p. 17.

not to have any of their own ...'[5] (He proves his point with exceptions to the rule such as Rembrandt's *Bathsheba* and *Danäe*.)

It seems to me that the statues next to Europe on the terrace of the Musée d'Orsay are statues of nude continents.

*   *   *

Early summer, early Sunday morning; Paris luminous in the slanting sunlight. The water in the gutters sparkles, flowing swiftly to clear the street of refuse from the night before. A short walk from Pigalle to Rochechouart through nearly empty streets. One or two locals, hardly dressed, are walking the dog or fetching a baguette. The Rue des Martyrs is slowly waking up to its weekly antique market—artwork and furniture, picture frames and bric-à-brac. An old Arab in a kaftan is drinking coffee in a pavement cafe. Another sits under a tree, just watching life go by. It's so beautiful! Paris, more than anywhere else in the world, tempts me as R S Thomas was tempted:

> ... One thing I have asked
> Of the disposer of the issues
> Of life: that truth should defer
> To beauty. It was not granted.[6]

When I lived in Paris I learned over the years to love and hate France as much as I love and hate Great Britain.

There is no concièrge at the entrance to the Chief Rabbi's apartment. It's Sunday and the door is locked, so I stand in the middle of the narrow street and call up to his window. It's an elegant stone building with a narrow balcony on each floor and wrought iron railings. The windows are open. He hears me and comes down to let me in. He's getting on now. In our conversation he speaks like the old European Jewish go-between, between Christians and Muslims, between the religions of the Book and Humanists. He is essentially a peacemaker, wise and modest. He tells me how he was struck to the ground in a Jerusalem street by a Jewish extremist who opposed his support for the peace process.

---

[5] John Berger, *Ways of Seeing*, BBC and Penguin Books, London, 1972, pp. 45-55.
[6] R S Thomas, *Petition*, in *Collected Works*, Phoenix, London, 1993, p. 209.

Lento sostenuto, dolce

In all beauty, a sadness
and a longing as in an alien land
MAKE IT NEW
(a new heaven and a new earth)[1]

One of the treasures of the National Museum in Warsaw, which has survived the centuries of warfare and looting that Polish art has had to suffer, is the statue of the Madonna of Wrocław. It was made in 1390, a sublime polychrome wooden sculpture of the virgin and child in the so-called Beautiful Style which came to dominate central European art at the turn of the fourteenth century. Crowned, and clothed in a long voluminous robe of blue, trimmed with gold, a young woman holds her child lightly on her arm. There is tenderness and pathos in her wide face. The child is naked and quite oblivious of his mother's watchful care, as she offers him the fruit Eve offered Adam in the garden. He takes it from her hand.

At the other end of the Royal Route from the museum, tucked away under trees in the corner of a park not far from the old city, is the statue of Our Lady of Passau. This madonna and child is a copy, sculpted in stone, of a painting by the school of Cranach, which was revered as the protectress against the plague (except that some ecclesiastical Philistine has plonked gilded metal crowns on their poor heads!). The plague reached its worst in Poland in 1625-26. But 1683, when the statue was made, was the date of liberation from another scourge—the Turks and Islam—which is why the monument was erected. Mary is wearing a sumptuous gown which comes down nearly to her ankles. Her hair falls to her shoulders, luxuriant. She holds the Christ child in her arms, a plump baby with the round face of a baroque cherub. He is naked, like the Gothic Christ in the museum, and stretches out his arms to his mother in a gesture of embrace. But she is not concerned with him. She is looking over his head to the city beyond.

---

[1] Ernesto Cardenal, 'Lines on the Death of Thomas Merton', in *Marilyn Monroe and other poems*, trans. Robert Pring-Mill, Search Press, London, 1975, p. 119.

Both statues are exquisite, yet as different as could be—the one which should be in a church and the other which is rightly in the street.

According to legend Luke the Evangelist was an artist. He had an eye for people, as did the unknown artist of the Madonna of Wrocław. 'There is a radiance in Luke's gospel,' Willy Barclay writes, 'which is a lovely thing, as if the sheen of heaven had touched the things of earth ...'[2] The same could be written of the Madonna of Wrocław. Her look and the innocence of the child on her arm are pure beauty.

As for Our Lady of Passau, when you think of what 1683 meant for Christian Europe, she had every reason to be distracted from her son's embraces. The Turkish siege of Vienna sent shock waves throughout Europe. A contemporary Ottoman chronicler tells how an Austrian prisoner, when questioned, reported 'that the Austrian emperor had sent letters to every side appealing for help to all the kings of Christendom, and that only the king of Poland, the accursed traitor called Sobieski, had come to his aid in person and with troops and with the soldiers and hetmans of Lithuania and with 35,000 cavalry and infantry of the Polish infidels.'[3] This was some show of strength, some 'shock of civilisations', as we would say today. You can imagine the Turks, those who survived, telling the story years later to their grandchildren, and calling it 'the mother and father' of all battles!

Given such a trauma, and such a deliverance—for Vienna, for Christendom, for Poland—it's not surprising that Warsaw has another much more obvious statue of Sobieski himself, in the Lazienki Park. It was unveiled a century after the Battle of Vienna. Sobieski is portrayed as a great Santiago Matamoros of the north, the victorious king riding a rampant horse, trampling two Turks. Larger than life, it stands on an arched bridge which closes the perspective of an ornamental lake in front of the Palace on the Water. The park is magnificent, with beautiful trees, lawns and flowerbeds, gazebos and orangeries—big enough to get lost in and far enough away from the Old Town and the ghetto to have survived the worst destruction of the war. Once when my wife and I were there, the peacocks were out

[2]   Willy Barclay, *The Gospel of Luke*, Saint Andrew Press, Edinburgh, 1975, p. 4.
[3]   Bernard Lewis, *The Muslim Discovery of Europe*, Phoenix, London, 1982, p. 41.

by the Palace on the Water, strutting and displaying and crying their eerie cries.

'In their own view of history, the Muslims were the bearers of God's truth with the sacred duty of bringing it to the rest of mankind,' writes Bernard Lewis. 'The House of Islam, of which they were a part, embodied God's purpose on earth. The sovereigns were the heirs of the Prophet and the custodians of the message which he had brought from God. The Islamic state was the only true legitimate power on earth and the Islamic community the sole repository of truth and enlightenment, surrounded on all sides by an outer darkness of barbarism and unbelief. God's favour to his own community was demonstrated by their power and their victories in this world. So it was and so it had always been since the days of the Prophet himself.'[4]

Our Lady of Passau had reason to be looking to the city. What a menace there was out there! It threatened the very foundations of Christendom. She was right, at least for now, to ignore the baby in her arms, even if all he wanted was a kiss.

*   *   *

The Church of the Holy Cross is on the Royal Route, more or less midway between the two madonnas. It is an imposing baroque church, built in the late seventeenth century Varsovian style, with a raised patio in front of the pillared main door and two great towers in its facade. Polish radio broadcasts mass from here every Sunday, which is an indication of its importance, both national and ecclesiastical, for the Poles. Chopin's heart is in a casket immured in a pillar in the nave, like the middle of a nocturne wrenched out of its three-part form. Beside it are words from the Sermon on the Mount: 'Where your treasure is, there will your heart be also.' By birth Friedrich Chopin was half French, half Polish, born about thirty miles away in Zelazowa Wola in 1810, though his family moved to Warsaw before he was one year old. He died in Paris in 1849, aged thirty-nine. The piano, that most European of all musical instruments, was a natural part of him, like an extension of his being.

In the early nineteen seventies the Dutch anarchist Roel van Duyn visited Edinburgh. He was a leader of two successive political

---

[4] *Op. cit.*, p. 39.

movements in Amsterdam, the *Provos* and the *Kabouters*, whose extraordinary social and environmental policies made quite a stir in the late sixties, when they were elected in force to the Amsterdam city council. In Edinburgh he was meeting students all day, and in the evening would come home tired to our house, sit down at the piano, and play Chopin. I remember his wistful, 'In heaven, there'll only be Chopin!'

*   *   *

The first settlement of Warsaw dates from the 10th century, though it was not until 1596 that King Zygmunt III Wasa transferred his royal residence and the main offices of state from Cracow to Warsaw. Half a century of feaverish activity by architects mostly from Italy added a series of Baroque buildings and resulted in an elegant city on the escarpment overlooking the great River Vistula. Warsaw became the intellectual hub of Central Europe. Its memory is preserved in etchings of the times. Zygmunt's Column which was erected in 1644 stands in the square in front of the castle, the oldest secular monument in the city. The king, his head crowned, and stooping, wears a cloak which is swept back over his right arm. In his right hand is a drawn scimitar, pointing forward, and in his left—as though he were a saint—a cross. But the Swedish invasion of Warsaw in 1655 was not far off and it was only the first of many catastrophes to befall the city.

There are not many trees in the Old Town of Warsaw, and those that there are, are all younger than me. However, compared to the seven hundred year old oak, Mieszko, on Nowoursenowska we are all mere saplings. Since the second world war, virtually the whole of the Old Town, something like a square mile of houses and shops, palaces and churches, has been rebuilt, resurrecting all the facades and stonework and jumbled roofs. When I visited Warsaw for the first time almost twenty years ago, the eighteenth century Royal Castle wasn't there. It had been destroyed in the war and its ruins cleared away. Now it's back again, rebuilt virtually as it was over two centuries ago. The architectural drawings which no longer existed were painstakingly reconstituted from a score of paintings from different viewpoints and perspectives, and from old photographs and archives retrieved from all over central Europe. It's an amazing story. The paintings, which had survived in hiding, and are once more hanging in an antechamber in the castle, are beautiful panoramas of the city by Bernard Belotto, who was called Canaletto after his uncle. The style is Canaletto's, except that it's Warsaw and not Venice.

Just off the Old Town Market Square, at the north end, up a little street called Waski Dunaj, there is an unimposing shop with a display of something or other in the rather grimy window. It's a small, low, shop front, opening directly on to the cobbled pavement. Inside are a number of cabinets and the remaining spaces on the walls are festooned with drawings of cut stones. My friend Staš greeted me in shorts and a singlet. He is a stone polisher and an intellectual, in his seventies now. Thirty years ago he was banned as a publisher and took up polishing gem stones to make a living. He still works part time with his son Peter and three employees in their cluttered workshop. Peter is the jeweller. Both father and son are ambidextrous. Working with both hands makes for a better technique, says Staš. Many of the Jewish jewellers and stone polishers in the ghetto were ambidextrous. As it was the feast of Saints Peter and Paul, I was invited into the workshop to celebrate Peter's name day, with coffee and open sandwiches and a glass of vodka tossed back in one.

A messenger from the trade came in with an order for Staš to cut two emerald gems for a wedding ring—1.7mm in diametre! He set in motion the polishing machine. He had designed and made it himself. The intricacy and detail of the work was astonishing. Afterwards he pulled out a box from the safe, and showed me a collection of cut stones—opals, rubies, emeralds, amethysts, I've forgotten the names of them all—an exquisite mix of nature and culture. One stone when he held it up to the artificial light was a translucent purple. In the daylight of the window it was blue and green and turquoise. Its name— alexandrite, a precious stone discovered two hundred years ago in Russia and named after the Czar. Polish alexandrite, Staš told me, fetches high prices in Japan.

As I was leaving he gave me two polished amber gems and a raw, uncut piece of Baltic amber for my wife.

*   *   *

The melody of the D flat Nocturne doesn't start immediately. Six-eight time, it opens like an annunciation, so quietly you can hardly hear it at all, with a full bar of triplets, twelve semi-quavers in the left hand, *Lento sostenuto*, to set the tempo and establish the key. That same underlying rhythm continues, *sempre legatissimo*, all the way through. Then you hear it—it almost takes you by surprise—a high F, *dolce*, ever so lightly (you play the note with the soft pad of the fourth finger of the right hand to give it the sweet singing tone it needs, changing to the fifth while the key is down, so as to have the other fingers free to carry on), a pure melodic line with a falling cadence, like a mother looking down at the baby in her arms. It starts with a dotted crochet, then a quaver, dotted quaver and semi-quaver, three steps down to the full octave and then up again immediately, to pause before three more light steps take it up to the high B flat. This B flat, a dotted crochet tied to a semi-quaver, has the kind of yearning in it which only finds relief when the melody moves it on. It tinkles down an octave once again, but not as might be expected to B flat, at least not yet. It's to the A natural immediately below it—to have to wait a whole bar, a dotted minim, on the interrupted cadence, still with the same accompaniment, before it eases itself voluptuously up to its resolution in the B flat.

Then comes the first bit of real Chopin, dancing up there like a tightrope walker dancing in the void, demi-semi-quavers and grace notes embellishing what feels as if it's almost too beautiful to bear already. The high note of this sequence is the high G flat octave. Its grace note, the note it jumps from to get up there, is the G flat an octave below. The effect is like that of the tightrope walker pausing ever so slightly to prepare himself for a leap. It's not that the technique is difficult (it's a black key played lightly with the side of the right hand thumb a split second before the little finger hits the dotted crochet an octave up, *forzando*); rather it is the emotional preparation which, if the leap to the high G flat is to succeed, requires that ever so brief moment of eternity.

This is the highest note of the nocturne so far. Apart from another grace note or two, and an extravaganza of rushing notes *con forza* later on, this tells us what the nocturne's all about. But there's no time to think about it. The music sparkles down in tiny droplets of grace notes, to a series of strong staccato semi-quavers, a down-to-earth left-right, left-right, all but one of them chromatic, up to the G natural. The interrupted cadence this time is above the note, resolving itself with a tiny flourish, like an intake of breath, on to the F. The *ten.* above the F stands for *tenuto*, i.e. the note should be sustained to the full value of its dotted crochet, perhaps even a trifle longer. That way you're ready for the *espressivo* which comes next ...

The coda, *dolcissimo*, is like little panting gestures, da-dum, da-dum, da-dum ..., a semi-tone down each time, and then repeated with the tiniest touch of a grace note to accompany each one, until finally, there's a series of consecutive fifths which mounts, languishing, like a young mum at the end of a long day tripping up the stairs to see why the baby's crying, right up to the high F double octave—a full two octaves above where the whole thing began! The resolution is *pianissimo*, not even a final cadence, just a restatement of the key. The nocturne's over. The baby's gone to sleep again.

Bruges
Time running out now
and the soul unfinished

> *... Time running out*
> *now, and the soul*
> *unfinished. And the heart knows*
> *this is not the portrait*
> *it posed for ...*
>
> R S Thomas, *Self-Portrait*

At the beginning of the 1990s, Jacques Delors, President of the European Commission, began to address the Christian churches and other religious and humanist communities in Europe in spiritual and ethical terms. His appeal was couched in eloquent phrases which caught the spirit of those years between 1989 and 1992, between the revolutions in the East and the completion of the Single Market in the West, when a sense of destiny surged once again into the popular European consciousness.

'We are in effect at a crossroads in the history of European construction,' he said, '1992 is a turning point. Even if on the surface of the sea nothing is yet visible, deep down the currents are beginning to change direction. The Maastricht summit marked the end of the economic phase of European construction, based on the drive towards the Common Market. We are now entering a fascinating time when the debate on the meaning of European construction becomes a major political factor. Believe me, we won't succeed with Europe solely on the basis of legal expertise or economic know-how. It is impossible to put the potential of Maastricht into practice without a breath of air. If in the next ten years we haven't managed to give a soul to Europe, to give it spirituality and meaning, the game will be up.

'This is why I want to revive the intellectual and spiritual debate on Europe. I invite the Churches to participate actively in it. The debate must be free and open. We don't want to control it; it's a democratic discussion, not to be monopolised by technocrats. I would like to create a meeting place, a space for free discussion open to men

---

[1] In *Laboratories of the Spirit*, Macmillan, London, 1975, p. 27.

and women of spirituality, to believers and non-believers, scientists and artists. We are working on the idea already ...'[2]

The response that this evoked on all sides was enthusiastic. The result was a flurry of activity leading eventually to the establishment of a fund of about three quarters of a million ECU per annum to subsidise projects which 'should promote reflection on the spiritual and/or ethical meaning of building a new Europe'. It was eventually called *A Soul for Europe: Ethics and Spirituality*. I was appointed as its first coordinator.

It is certainly a rewarding job to work with grass-roots groups of believers across the length and breadth of Europe—local mosques searching for a European Muslim identity, student Christian movements committed to understanding how the global economy works, inter-faith responses to the Ecumenical Patriarch's call for a new theology of creation. Their efforts often seem to fit the original purpose of the European Community better than more official programmes. But, when it comes to the consequences of such reflection which Jacques Delors implied was relevant to the European Commission, I wonder whether the institution, such as it is, is capable of taking them on board. Understandably, officials often speak a double language in these matters— on the one hand, what they themselves believe and, on the other, what the institution obliges them to do. With values like peace, unity, democracy, freedom of religion, there is little disagreement. But, by definition, a modern, secular, political institution cannot be expected to accommodate religious presuppositions. What then might the ethical contribution of grass-roots religious associations mean in the sphere of institutional economics and technology? How can spirituality influence bureaucracy?

Shortly before his death, Bishop Leslie Newbigin wrote this comment on a European Commission memorandum entitled *The Vocation of Europe*: 'Talk about ethical and moral values is empty if it is not based on some view of what is the case. It is, in fact, one of the sure signs of a culture in terminal decline when it begins to talk about the need for moral values ... We cannot decide to "have a new economic system" or "promote morality" simply because these would be desirable. These things cannot be detached from the total belief-system which governs public life.'[3]

---

[2] *Newsletter* of the Ecumenical Centre, Brussels, No. 2, May 1992, p. 1.

[3] Personal correspondence.

The danger of ethical and spiritual discussion within political and economic institutions, when it is promoted officially, is that it may lead to a further mystification of reality. It becomes a formality that confers legitimacy where it is intrinsically lacking. Economics throws a shadow over ethics which can falsify the dialogue.

According to Ivan Illich, ethics—in a long tradition going back to Aristotle—was a public controversy about the good, to be pursued, perhaps grudgingly, within the confines of the human condition. Economics, on the other hand, is built on the assumption of scarcity. It deals with statistics, calculations and goals, and so tends to relativise ethics, reducing it to its own terms. Progress and development set out to pursue the better at the expense of the good. Economic society 'provides seemingly unlimited fuel for a technological civilisation,' while 'such a civilisation attempts to transform the human condition, rather than debate the nature of the human good.'[4]

The concept of value, likewise, used to denote what was useful and desirable within a specific cultural context. But values in a secular institutional context are a measure that matches the abstract ideology of economics. This does not imply that values no longer have any meaning, but rather that their meaning is influenced by an economic system which dominates and distorts reality. In an institutional context, there is no stable criterion for choice between them—nor indeed for choice between what is a value and what is not.

A Soul for Europe: Ethics and Spirituality offers grassroots groups an opportunity to develop a critique of European Union policy along such lines. The European Union desperately needs it, but doesn't like it, or doesn't care. At the institutional level, particularly in matters of economics and technology, the critique has to be *counter-cultural*. I believe that Jacques Delors realised this though his senior advisers for the most part never acknowledged it.

*　　　*　　　*

Not far from the Grande Place of Bruges is the Bridge of St John of Nepomuk, the protector of bridges. Punts and tourist barges pass up and down the canal beneath it. Old creeper-covered red brick walls

---

[4] Ivan D Illich, *The Wisdom of Leopold Kohr*, Bremen, 1996, duplicated paper, p. 5.

stretch along one side of the canal as you look south-westwards. On the other side there is the Dijver, a broad wharf lined with great lime-trees. On Saturdays and Sundays in the summer months a flea market crams the space between the trees with antiques and bric-à-brac. An elegant fifteenth century mansion originally used to store 'grut', a mixture of dried flowers, plants and barley for brewing beer, overlooks another ancient bridge at the far end of the wharf. It is now the Gruuthuse Museum, packed with exhibits of Flemish furniture, decorative arts, weapons and lace. Most beautiful is a painted wooden bust of the young Emperor Charles V, sculpted to mark his visit to Bruges in 1520, though by then Bruges was already a city in decline.

I've stood on the Dijver on Ascension Day to watch the Procession of the Holy Blood, the annual pageant of Bruges. It commemorates the relic of the blood of Christ which, according to tradition, was brought to Bruges in 1150 by Thierry of Alsace, Count of Flanders, on his return from the second crusade. The spectacular procession has fifty scenes or floats and involves two thousand of the citizens of Bruges and hundreds of animals, from dogs to dromedaries. It is divided into four parts, the main scenes of which are brief mystery plays enacted repeatedly for the crowds of onlookers along the way: the Old Testament (paradise lost, the call of Abraham, Joseph and his brothers, the prophets and the Ark), the New Testament (scenes from the life of Jesus), Thierry and his knights bringing the relic from Jerusalem, and finally the shrine itself surrounded by the Noble Brotherhood of the Holy Blood with today's clerical and civic authorities. The golden shrine, which is carried by two prelates, houses the phial of blood in a costly reliquary. Amongst the other priceless treasures it contains is a large black diamond, the gift of Mary Queen of Scots.

Behind the Dijver, in a courtyard, is the famous Groeninge Museum with some of the best paintings of the Flemish Primitives. Beyond it, hiding the twelfth century Hospice of St John, now the Memling Museum, rises the tower and spire of the thirteenth century Church of Notre-Dame. There the young Michelangelo's exquisite sculpture of the Virgin and Child adorns a side altar. Its bronze copy in St Cuthbert's Church in Edinburgh lacks the luminosity of the original's white marble and the calm, young, thoughtful beauty of the Virgin's face!

In the midst of all this stands the College of Europe, a long white building overlooking the Dijver.

*   *   *

I was attending a conference with clergy and laity from a couple of Anglican dioceses in southern England at a centre in the Netherlands, just over the border from Bruges. The opening lecture by a Dutch theologian was entitled 'Heart and Soul of Europe'; this was followed by an illustrated talk from a local art historian on 'The Language of the Flemish Primitives'; then came a presentation by me on 'Europe in Search of Meaning'. Finally on the following morning there was a visit to the College of Europe where the Rector, Dr Otto von der Gablentz, was to give a speech entitled 'A Soul for Europe'.

Dr von der Gablentz was introduced by the conference leader as 'one of the great Europeans of our time'. A German with perfect English and French, he was his country's ambassador to the Netherlands, Israel and Russia before becoming rector of the College of Europe in 1995. He received us graciously. At the beginning of the lecture he redefined his subject: instead of 'A Soul for Europe' he would speak about 'Having responsible European citizens', which for him, he said, meant the same thing.

The Rector began with a brief survey of the history and background of the College of Europe. It is the oldest institute of European studies in the continent, dating back to 1948 and The Hague conference which laid the basis for the Council of Europe. European institutions need Europeans, and it was the Spanish statesman and exile, Salvador de Madariaga, who, recognising this, led the way to establishing a college for the purpose of training students to face up to the challenges of European integration. This gave rise to what was famously called *l'esprit de Bruges,* the spirit of Bruges.

(Salvador de Madariaga represents an age in European affairs when there was a real sense of purpose and vocation, as these famous lines of his suggest:

> Above all we must love Europe ... this Europe must be born. And she will, when Spaniards will say 'our Chartres', and Englishmen 'our Cracow', the Italians 'our Copenhagen'; when Germans say 'our Bruges', and step back horror-striken at the idea of laying murderous hands on it. Then will Europe live, for then it will be

that the Spirit that leads History will have uttered the creative words: Fiat Europa!)[5]

The moment when universities could play an integrating role in Europe is long past now. Dr von der Gablentz began to focus on his theme. University reform in the 1950s was all done at national level. A great opportunity thus was lost. It should have been undertaken internationally. Thinking the European dimension has nevertheless always been the aim of the College of Bruges, however limited its means. Its task is to be leadership training, an '*école de cadres* to man the institutions', on the French model of the *école nationale d'administration*.

University graduates from different countries live and study together. Academic work in French and English covers four principal departments: economics, human resources development, law, and political and administrative sciences. Courses began in the 1950s with less than thirty students. Now there are 270 graduate students representing 32 different countries. It's a microcosm of Europe. Because of the competition for places, the students are the *crème de la crème*. A second campus was opened in Natolin (Warsaw) in 1994.

Three times during his talk Dr von der Gablentz spoke of 'the Achilles heel of European construction' to describe the lack of European consciousness amongst European citizens, indeed their ignorance and apathy about the fact that, since Maastricht, they *are* European citizens. The political context has radically changed since the College was founded. The importance of the nation state has progressively lost its exclusivity. 70 percent of the laws affecting citizens today are European Union-based. Sovereignty, defined as 'the monopoly of power in one place', is a dead word. The eternal significance De Gaulle bequeathed to the nation state is nonsense in the light of history. The European Union, as an effort to master 'the uncontrollability of our world', is miles away from that. Yet only a fraction of the GNP of the combined member states is vested in the EU. Sixteen or seventeen thousand civil servants—less than the numbers employed by a single large European city—are all the employees it has. The European Union is 'an open-ended process of reform, not a new federation or confederation like the United States of America'.

---

[5] Salvador de Madariaga, *Portrait of Europe*, Hollis and Carter, London, 1952, p. 3.

The Achilles heel of Europe, this lack of a basis in the hearts and minds of European citizens, makes it possible for 'Europe' to be used as a scapegoat by politicians. What is needed is political leaders who will not undermine Europe at the first opportunity.

So far Dr von der Gablentz could almost have stuck to the title 'A Soul for Europe'. But what, he went on to ask, is to be done?

Soft ware, hard ware and wet ware (brains) are what counts. Increasingly we depend on brain power today; not on industry. There is a danger of exclusion—30-40 percent of citizens are incapacitated in this new situation. Life-long learning—education and training—are the moving factor for the future. The real task from now on is to build up common concepts for the knowledge society. It will be a different society, and a new social challenge will be formulated as it comes into place—a knowledge society with a European dimension. To underline his point, he quoted Professor Henri Brugmans, the first Rector of the College: 'We need to revive our European civilisation by the shock of political union.'

But how is this to be done given the state of education in the Union? Take Germany and Belgium: there are altogether twenty different Ministries of Education in the two national governments, the German Länder and the Belgian regions. Educational guidelines for the knowledge society are essential at European level. But each wants to defend the cultural values of its own region, to which education is so closely linked. This is to 'undermine Europe'. Since the Commission has no competence in the field of education, it has to find other ways of doing what it thinks is necessary. The Rector went on to elaborate the kind of training policy represented by the hi-tech, industry-related, long-distance learning policy of the Commission—it can simply bypass the education ministries of national and regional governments. Let's be pragmatic, he said, this is the way to create 'a soul for Europe'.

He finished speaking. There was a pause. The first question from the floor came from someone who was concerned about what ordinary people might want, whether or not they recognise that they are European citizens: how did he take into account their wishes? Otto von der Gablentz's reply was swift and breathtaking: 'The world is so complicated that people cannot know what they want. We have to decide for them.' Another question related to what he had said about the German and Belgian ministries of education, to which he replied: 'If left to the educationalists, they will make a mess of it.'

I, being Brussels based and involved with *A Soul for Europe*, was invited to ask the last question. I didn't particularly want to. I think the conference organiser may have expected a vote of thanks! It seemed to me, I said, that Dr von der Gablentz's knowledge society was being promoted as the junior partner of big business. And in promoting it the European Union was aligning itself not only with big business, but also with a reductionist approach to the future. What about democracy and freedom? What about the diversity of Europe and the multiple, creative identities of its peoples and citizens?

*   *   *

In 1936-37 Eugen Rosenstock-Huessy wrote his great history of Europe, *Out of Revolution: Autobiography of Western Man*.[6] It was the year of the tercentenary of Descartes' *Discourse on Method*, and Rosenstock ends his book by turning one last time to 'the venerable Descartes, our adversary, the great seducer of the modern world.'[7]

He willingly acknowledges that Descartes' *Cogito ergo sum* opened the way to three hundred years of incredible scientific progress. But his attack on Cartesianism 'is inevitable since "pure" thought encroaches everywhere on the field of social sciences'. Historians, psychologists, economists cannot stand the idea of not being pure thinkers, real scientists. How frustrating! 'I am an impure thinker,' Rosenstock writes, 'I am hurt, swayed, shaken, elated, disillusioned, shocked, comforted, and I have to transmit my mental experiences lest I die. Although I may die ...'

The vigorous identity required of us by the *Cogito ergo sum* tends to destroy the guiding imperatives of the good life. 'We do not exist because we think. Man is the son of God and not brought into being by thinking. We are called into society by a mighty entreaty, "Who art *thou*, man, that I should care for thee?" ... "Man" is the *second person* in the grammar of society.'[8]

Rosenstock's voice, and others like it, need to be heard today, not least in the College of Europe. He asks the question 'what the

---

[6] Eugen Rosenstock-Huessy, *Out of Revolution: Autobiography of Western Man*, Argo Books, Norwich, Vt., 1938 and 1969.

[7] *Op. cit.*, p. 754.

[8] *Op. cit.*, p. 748.

omission of laughter, or its application, mean in the evolution of science ... (for) a man who fails to apply laughter and weeping in the discovery of vital truth simply is immature ...'[9]

'Tell me,' he says, 'how far you share responsibility with the blunderers of the past, and when you have shown me to what extent you are capable of identification with the rest of mankind, I shall know whether your knowledge is survival knowledge ...'[10]

---

[9] *Op. cit.*, p. 754.
[10] *Op. cit.*, p. 758.

Scrabster

Standing at the edge

Scrabster, or Skarabolstadr in old Norse,
means (as I learned)
the standing at the edge.

There in that harbour on the north
coast of Scotland, facing
the awful power of the Pentland Firth
and the North Atlantic,
you inhale a certain metaphysic—
an exhilarating liberation
(if the gale doesn't blow you over)
from the centripetal force
of our monstrous civilisation.

It's not the call of the unknown
that made bold sailors quit
the safety of the old continent in frail
caravels five centuries ago.
It's not the curious economy of surface—
the globe and our flat knowledge of it—
that confronts the mystic on the shores of
California, gazing westwards towards the east.
The ocean here conveys a more immediate,
elementary intelligence.

For all the efforts of technology to resist
the limits and authority of nature,
the sea yet marks an end to the land,
to continuity, to the place of our
endeavours—at the end of the day, to culture.
It reminds the willing imagination of that
necessary humility, without which
human constructs are vain.

Nature and time, as they are in
Scrabster, won't be coopted.
They're not partisans of Holyrood,
or Westminster or Brussels.
The sea and the sky and the sound
of sheer silence are an intimation at the edge
of Europe that there's a term to the arrogance
and menace of the Western world.

The wind blows steadily over
Scrabster's cliffs—contradicting the din
of the ten lanes of traffic on the boulevard
where I live. The wind
blows where it wills, and high above
there are the gannets, soaring, watchful,
diving with a desperate hope
against air and sea, worrying a sombre sky
with their stark white purity.

Part Two

All we ever have is here, now

We are strangers in the cosmos tourists really
having no dwelling here but just hotels
Ernesto Cardenal, *Lines on the Death of Thomas Merton.*

*   *   *

The difficulty of translation from a language that doesn't yet exist is
considerable, but there's no need to exaggerate it. The past, after all,
can be quite as obscure as the future ... All we ever have is here, now.
Ursula Le Guin, *Always coming home.*

What's it all about?

The journey from Taynuilt took us down Loch Awe through Kilchrenan and Inverinan, via Lochavich to the Firth of Lorn. Continuing over the Atlantic Bridge we came to Seil Island, and Easdale with its rows of low quarriers' houses huddled against the elements. The bleak slate quarries are abandoned now, their deep pits filled with dark water. Once they roofed the Western Isles, sheltered the heads of monk and crofter from the stern blast of an inclement sky's savage preaching. To the south we could see the full force of the Atlantic breaking on Cullipool's rocks.

On Iona the Abbey Trustees' master mason explained to me the pointing of the Abbey walls and the different techniques used to combat the relentless wind and driving rain. When I asked how long the job would take, he shrugged and replied that he hoped it would see him through his working life. He was middle-aged.

Behind St Oran's Chapel, where the summer pilgrimages round the island end, is my father's grave. 'You don't belong anywhere,' says Gabriel Garcia Marquez in *One Hundred Years of Solitude,* 'so long as you haven't any dead under the ground.' The November day we carried my father's coffin from the parish church to the graveyard of the kings, was clear and sharp and cold, and but for a veil of mist on the summit of Ben More, the sky was cloudless.

The road north from Connel through Benderloch and along Loch Creran follows the old railway line in places. Its rails were lifted years ago, but the embankments and cuttings remain. Retaining walls and arches still witness to the skilled masons who constructed them. There are those who would like it back, but the railway has long been beyond replacement. Where locomotives used to steam and hiss, the way now is overgrown with birch and whin. A group of holiday chalets has been built right on the line. It will not carry passengers again.

Roland Walls was for ever peppering his divinity lectures at New College with the question, 'What's it all about?' If discussion about the nature of the church is to be significant, it must pose probing questions about our manner of doing things, about the relation between establishment and exclusion, professionalism and lack of volunteers, a management mentality and the loss of spirituality, scarce resources and the dearth of free spirits.

'What's it all about?' is essentially the same question whether it is posed at the centre of European affairs or at the periphery. The impression of a world without meaning, the sense of loss, is equally grievous whether it is to do with the uncertainty following the collapse of the Soviet Union and the end of the Cold War, or the inexorable depopulation of beautiful Glengarry. Confidence has been eroded in any over-arching worldview—be it the Bible story, political ideology or the cultural patterns of a locality—which might make sense of history and explain the changes which impinge so sharply on our lives.

In Brussels recently I sat in on a meeting between the Moderator, Dr James Simpson, and the UK Permanent Representative to the European Union, Sir John Kerr. They had a good 'gossip' about theology and life, as the Ambassador put it later. He reminisced about holidays as a child in Speyside with his grandfather, A J Gossip, Professor of Divinity at Glasgow University, while the Moderator remembered Professor Gossip's sermons.

In Foyers Manse overlooking Loch Ness I came across a collection of Gossip's sermons. They have not lost their resonance.

> Many, even after years of pottering about this business (religion), seem to have never a notion of the real meaning and the fundamental purpose of the thing …There are those who are accounted religious, who are not religious, but mere spiritual hypochondriacs, for ever fingering their own spiritual pulse …
>
> It is *the* problem of life,' said Marcus Dods in his frank way, 'why does Christianity do so little for men?'… what dreams God has dreamed for you and me! What sacrifices he has made on our behalf! … And this is all there is to show, even for Calvary! The whole stupendous enginery of grace has so far effected in us only this preposterously meagre output! There is something wrong …
>
> (But) before we leap up and set off again more purposefully, and at a mended pace, we must make certain

we are travelling in the right direction. For it is not enough
to have the feeling that something must be done ...[1]

At the evening service in a housing estate near Oban, the
minister, a conservative evangelical, had invited two Faith Mission
evangelists to give their testimonies, I suppose to balance the fact that
I was preaching. They were engaged in a local mission and staying in a
caravan at the back of the church. They made their witness, earnest
young men—a Scot with a PhD in archaeology, and a former electrician
from Northern Ireland, both in their mid-twenties. I couldn't help but
admire their courage in standing up before a congregation and speaking
so personally about themselves and their faith. But beyond the tight
circle of salvation surrounding each of them there was little of
theological substance in what they had to say. 'Watchman,' asks the
prophet, not 'how are you feeling?' but 'what of the night?'

The session clerk in Taynuilt was a retired forester with a lot
of patience, and a face that looked as if it had been carved out of the
rock of ages. On the Sunday I was there his wife, the organist, got an
elderly Highland church choir to teach the congregation to sing a new
Wild Goose version of Psalm 8 to the old tune of 'Tramps and
Hawkers':

> When I look up, and see the stars ...
>
> then must I ask, 'Why do you care?
> Why love humanity?
> And why keep every mortal name
> fixed in your memory?'
>
> Yet such as us you made and meant
> just less than gods to be ...[2]

What's it all about? There and then, it seemed to make some sense. I
caught a glimpse in Taynuilt of the holy, catholic church!

---

[1] A J Gossip, *From the Edge of the Crowd*, T & T Clark, Edinburgh, 1956, pp. 15, 21.

[2] No. 8, *Psalms of Patience, Protest and Praise*, Wild Goose, 1994.

*   *   *

Not long before leaving Belgium, we went to see the Béjart Ballet in a performance entitled *King Lear—Prospero,* an extraordinary, free interpretation of two Shakespearean plays together, one after the other. Its unity came from the treatment of the relationship between a father and a daughter in Lear and Cordelia, Prospero and Miranda. The piece was eclectic in a quite uninhibited way, blending ballet and theatre, circus and mime in a powerful evocation of the drama, which was being performed outside, of Europe after the Cold War.

Europe, it reminded you, is not just a geographical entity—a patchwork of nations and cultures on the western edge of Asia—but a crucible of civilisation. And this civilisation is again today confronted with rupture and the end of empire. Fundamental questions are being raised once more: about power, madness, meaninglessness, death (*King Lear*); and enchantment, surprise, celebration, purpose (*The Tempest*). 'Art which stays news ... is art in which the question "what does it mean?" has no correct answer.' (Tom Stoppard)

The first act, from the initial division of the kingdom to the final scene strewn with corpses, was a *dance macabre:* death, the chorus, was the hero. The ballet in which Lear takes the dead Cordelia in his arms is the climax of the tragedy: how the life-giving spirit of a young girl can be destroyed by the arrogance and stupidity of her father. Though, in the moment when Lear holds his daughter's lifeless body in his arms, you glimpse the mirror image of another drama, another *pietà,* where a mother clasps her dead son to herself and the grief and dereliction of the world await redemption.

The second act was set in a great circus ring that filled the stage: a vital performance where the struggle between good and evil was overwhelmed by the magic of life. The music was cosmopolitan, words and mime and gobbledegook all part of the show. The same tragic figure who portrayed the power and madness of the old King Lear now played the fatherly magician Prospero.

The finale of Prospero involved the whole *corps de ballet* dancing their hearts out to a medley of 1930s cabaret songs, when suddenly in from the back comes the figure of the blinded Gloucester of the other play, his empty eye-sockets still covered with a bloody cloth, one hand on his son Edgar's shoulder, the other reaching out into the void. As Prospero finally renounces his magic and accepts that his daughter

will leave him for her lover, Gloucester shuffles through the dancers
and falls to his knees in the foreground. When the stage clears, only
Gloucester (representing Lear) and Prospero, are left—a stark
alternative—and a voice, reminding us that

> ... We are such stuff
> As dreams are made on, and our little life
> Is rounded with a sleep.

*   *   *

Boleskine Church on a clear cold Sunday morning—a small, simple,
two-hundred-year-old Highland kirk on the side of Stratherrick, its
windows looking over to Loch Mhór and Lochgarthside—light
everywhere on the soft colours of winter's ending, the wind still like
a knife ('No midges today!' said the elder at the door), one solitary
crow measuring the distance to the far side of the strath: the Word
of God seemed to be in place here, natural, congruous, inviting
hesitant hearts to give in to the spirit of the wind, coursing over the
magnificent land.

Later that morning in Dores, a nineteenth century parish church
at the head of Loch Ness, too big now and seeming emptier for the
presence of not twenty of a congregation at the back: hardened old
sinner that I am, I have a mystical double-take in the pulpit that brings
tears jerking to my eyes as the minister reads the Great Dialogue—the
story of Jesus and Nicodemus—and thin voices sing Laurence
Housman's tremendous hymn which echoes down this terrible century,
corroborating what we too know of history:

> Races and peoples, lo! we stand divided
> And sharing not our griefs no joy can share; ...
>
> In wrath and fear, by jealousies surrounded,
> Building proud towers which shall not reach to heaven
>
> Led by no star, the rulers of the nations
> Still fail to bring us to the blissful birth.

Yet, compellingly, irrefutably, overwhelmingly,

> How shall we love thee, holy, hidden Being,
> If we love not the world which Thou hast made?[3]

---

[3] Laurence Housman, Hymn No. 507, *The Church Hymnary*, Third Edition, OUP, Oxford, 1973.

St Leonard's Well

High smooth grey clouds with a girdle of radiance gave the sky the appearance of raw silk. There were birds everywhere: curlews feeding in stubble fields, peewits with their awkward, crumpled flight, rackety rooks in tall bare trees, hawks perched on barnyard roofs, gulls wheeling overhead (wheeling, wheeling, then suddenly gone), a lone cormorant hurrying over the face of the sea, its long neck straining towards some urgent assignation. And regularly at dusk and dawn, the fundamental rhythm of nature, *grazioso e giocoso*, in the swaying V formations of the wild geese flying from the Eden estuary to the Cameron reservoir, from the Cameron reservoir to the Eden estuary, as they always did at this time of year

Whichever way you come upon St Andrews—from Guardbridge or Strathkinness, the Kinkell Braes, the Grange or over the hill from Largo—the view of the town is lovely, calm and reassuring. Distant towers and spires, slate roofs and grey stone walls stand firm and solid, waiting for you, as they have patiently awaited travellers for well nigh a thousand years. I would have preferred to walk the last few miles into town, to allow for time to arrive.

The ancient city is built on a headland jutting out into a wide bay of the North Sea, flanked by cliffs and beaches, links and dunes. Sailing in by boat is the best way to arrive—the way Saint Regulus arrived in the fifth century, or Hexham's Bishop Acca in the eighth, Mary Queen of Scots rounding the coast from Edinburgh or John Knox returning from exile in France. It was the route taken by countless travellers until the introduction of roads in the eighteenth and nineteenth centuries gradually overcame the frustrations of inland travel.

Once, as a boy, I sailed into St Andrews in my brother's Dysart yawl. A stout following wind from the east filling the lugsail's patched, red, faded canvas. Ropes taut, timbers creaking with the strain, the sea's smell, and the sense of stillness and speed which the sea wind shares with the sailor. Rollers swirling past the undecked gunwales as we overtook or fell behind the swell. Racing straight in under the braes to the white bar of the East Sands and, beneath the ruined cathedral, the harbour hidden behind its piers.

Some say that in mediaeval times St Andrews was more celebrated than Canterbury as a place of pilgrimage in Northern Europe. In the whole of Western Christendom it was second only to Santiago de Compostela. Returning crusaders who compared its topography to the Holy City called it the Jerusalem of the North.

Andrew was the first of Jesus' disciples, according to John's Gospel. It was he who introduced his brother, Simon Peter, to our Lord. According to Mark and Matthew, Peter and Andrew were the first to be called, together. Like the sons of Zebedee, they were Galilean fishermen. It's strange that Andrew wasn't there with the others, Peter, James and John, to witness the transfiguration or sit with Jesus in Gethsemane.

St Andrew was crucified in Patras in Greece in 65 A.D. and his embalmed body, so the story goes, was carried from Patras to Constantinople in the fourth century, to Rome in bits and pieces in the sixth, Canterbury and Hexham in the seventh, and finally, by some accounts, to St Andrews in the year 732. A few relics were all that remained for the final journey. But well before the end of the first millennium, the former Kilrymont, the 'church on the mount of the kings', had adopted his name. After forcing a north-west passage, like an arm of his cross across Europe, the saint found a resting place at last.

Unlike St James, the patron saint of Spain who joined the ecclesiastical foreign legion and was enlisted by the Conquistadors, Andrew stayed put in Scotland. He did a lot less harm that way, playing a supportive cultic role in his decrepitude, until the Reformers did away with saints and pilgrimage. But not before his relics had inspired some of the most magnificent Scottish architecture of the Middle Ages.

Begun in 1160, St Andrews cathedral took a century and a half to build. All the time of the Scottish Wars of Independence it provided another, complementary expression of national sentiment. It was completed in 1318, four years after the Battle of Bannockburn, at a time when a tide was turning in the affairs of Scotland. Robert the Bruce was there for its consecration.

'It was the largest building ever constructed in Scotland,' says Jurek Putter, 'until the Victorians ... began building their enormous hotels, hospitals and railway stations.'

I called on Jurek in his artist's studio up a close on South Street, and talked to him for an hour or so. We were at school together.

His passionate research in support of his interpretation of the past, and his intricately detailed pencil drawings of St Andrews have for many years drawn attention to the city as he maintains it was in the Middle Ages. His work is a fascinating, eccentric attempt by a fervent Roman Catholic to provide a substitute—if one can imagine calling it that, at such a remove—for a certain form of religious art that he believes was almost all destroyed at the Reformation. According to Putter, they were 'travelling pictures', oil paintings on wooden panels, measuring as much as eleven by seven feet, commissioned by wealthy patrons to tour Scotland 'in their own little theatres on wheels'. They were accompanied by a mendicant priest who made it his lifetime's vocation 'to reach scattered communities, taking to them a powerful, eloquent and enduring image of the Scottish Heartlands, that otherwise would only have existed in the oral tradition.' *St Andrews—The Pilgrim City 1460 AD* is an encyclopaedic panorama of the city, a bird's eye view, including the southern wall of the city, the Cathedral complex, houses and riggs, and beyond it all St Andrews Bay, the hills of Angus and the Grampians.

Paris had to await Haussmann's new town planning, which followed the destruction caused by the Commune, to have such boulevards as St Andrews' mediaeval North and South Streets. They were conceived as broad pilgrim ways, converging in the east before the cathedral. Its vast structure, sitting on the headland above the cliffs, was a landmark for sailors for more than two centuries. Below it, the long grey sandstone pier unwound itself warily into the sea.

*   *   *

On the Sunday I was in St Andrews I preached to a full congregation in Hope Park, my father's old church. This was where I spent my childhood—a solid, informed, concerned, establishment congregation; little seemed to have changed. The elegant canopied pulpit, salvaged by my father and his architect elders from Thomas Chalmers' West Port Church in Edinburgh, the fine embroidered communion tablecloth on the large table he installed, the Victorian stained glass window above the gallery that dominated the perspective from the manse pew: the patriarch Abraham, his knife raised over his son's breast, authority and duty sentimentally combined, with a mother-figure angel interrupting, pointing to the ram caught in the thicket, watching, waiting.

'Don't you remember me?' asks an aged dear, but (I'm sorry) I haven't a clue. Or again, 'I was your first Sunday School teacher,' and he hardly seems to have changed a bit! The small talk at the door of the church a distraction from the grand emotion that should have broken but never did to mark the occasion.

On the Monday morning I addressed the St Leonard's School Assembly—several hundred girls in green (their uniform used to be brown)—on hope and reconciliation. Unfolding a European map I bought in Auschwitz, the town in the centre of Europe where, as Hitler discovered, all the railway lines converged, I talked about the Second World War, the European Union, Cold War and the end of empire. There were two girls from Poland there. Afterwards the headmistress in an elegant gown served me coffee in her study overlooking gardens where Mary Stuart walked, and talked to me about the school, and about ballet, the Baltic States and Ricky Demarco's Europe.

As I left, a girl was playing the organ in St Leonard's Chapel, tucked away behind the Pends, the mediaeval gateway to the town. On winter evenings prayers were said there by candlelight, the students wrapped in their thick red undergraduate gowns. Patrick Hamilton, George Wishart, Walter Myln, all 'drank of St Leonard's Well', as it was said—the fresh water of theology from Germany, Switzerland, Flanders, France and England—and paid for it with their lives. Here the Scottish Reformation began, marking the beginning of the end of St Andrews as it had been—the resplendent, utterly decadent, ecclesiastical 'golden age' of the century leading up to 1560. The chapel, the college, a church, and the public school are all that remain of the name of St Leonard.

Not to be talking to you about God

The old crofter who drove me from Broadford to Portree pointed out the township where he was born, the route the main road used to take, the jetty for the new Raasay ferries. 'I've worked with engines all my life,' he told me, nodding towards the Sound. He was an engineer on coastal vessels of the Royal Navy, recovering stray missiles and torpedoes from the seabed at the nearby practice range in the Minch. He still did some crofting. When I remarked on what seemed to me his good health, he told me he had recently had a heart attack from which he only recovered after coming across a text from Psalm 41 by chance: 'The Lord sustains him on his sickbed; in his illness thou healest all his infirmities.'

Strange that a line from a psalm written so long ago and so far away, should have such an immediate impact on an old man's health today. The Bible still speaks to people though the prevailing culture may have little room for it. The minister who arranged my visit to the school in Portree thought it necessary to advise me to avoid any suggestion of religion in the classroom. I used my maps and cartoons to get the children talking about Europe down the centuries. The Hereford Cathedral *mappa mundi* is a powerful expression of the world view of mediaeval Christendom, but its religious impact eight centuries later isn't controversial. And the wordless cartoons of Selçuk Demirel from *Le Monde Diplomatique* which throw up questions about globalisation, information technology and the free market, might be regarded as prophetic by the likes of me, but that's because what they expose is the false religion of our times.

In the manse across the road I had tea with the Portree minister and his family. They were Gaelic speakers from Uist. The son had taken a year off studying at Aberdeen University and was working locally as a window cleaner. He was cleaning the manse windows when I arrived, a delightful, irrepressible young man—and a good photographer. He showed me a photograph he had taken of a sea eagle being harried by a crow in flight across the bay. His sister, in her first year at Glasgow University, was home for Easter—a gentle, timid, pretty girl. She set aside her diffidence at my presence to enjoy being with her brother again and laugh at his jokes. How wonderful, I thought, for him! I was a guest, a stranger in the household: I knew nothing of the family's joys and sorrows, hopes or disappointments. But it didn't matter. Tired from the long day's work and travel, I let go, sat back, drank my tea, and for a lovely moment enjoyed these two young people, listened to their silly talk and laughter, and joined in their father's quiet, unobtrusive admiration.

The rector of Plockton High School took me round the school and introduced me to various classes, teachers and pupils, before the assembly I was to address. The school was well informed about European affairs. A higher history course was coming to an end; there were posters on the classroom walls covering subjects like the First World War and apartheid in South Africa, but also the local history of Wester Ross and the Highland Clearances. We got talking, the history teacher and I, about changes in the curriculum in recent years, and how the emphasis now is more on particularity and diversity. The predominant, national, centrist, unifying approach to history of the past has been abandoned.

Angus Peter Campbell, writer-in-residence at the Gaelic College on Skye, in his second book of poems, includes this bitter reflection about past methods of schooling and history teaching in Scotland:

. . .

as if it was like hammering nails into wood.

55 BC Julius Caesar invaded Britain
AD 80 Julius Agricolla led the Romans into Scotland
563 St Columba came to Iona
844 Kenneth MacAlpine became King over Dalriada,
     Pictland, Lothian and Strathclyde
1263 The Battle of Largs; The Hebrides became Scottish
1314 The Battle of Bannockburn
1513 The Battle of Flodden
1542 The Battle of Solway Moss; Mary Queen of Scots
     born
1560 Treaty of Leith
1587 The execution of Mary Queen of Scots
1588 The Spanish Armada
1603 The Union of the Crowns
1707 The Union of Parliaments

At which point Scottish history came to an end,
as if it had no connection with anything,
least of all with itself.

Millions of Highers, millions of graduates ...[1]

At a recent seminar on the information society which I had
attended in Brussels, organised by the European Commission, a lecturer
in Law at the University of Louvain spoke about the Internet in terms
relevant to history teaching as well:

> All the policies being developed now are formulated in
> a rhetoric and jargon which focuses on the local, the
> situational, the contextual, the face-to-face. While, on
> the one hand, systems are constructing an inaccessible
> and highly technical language on values, society seems
> to be reacting by turning to the personal, the authentic
> and the local in order to preserve a certain ability—
> despite a situation of extreme alienation—to construct
> identities which, while they are fragile and precarious,
> are nevertheless desired and individualized. The return
> to authoritarian or interventionist policies ... can only
> falter in a world which is opening up, where systems
> are self-regulating and where culture is ceasing to
> function in a central manner. We must therefore invent
> new institutions ...[2]

Centrifugal and centripetal forces are at work in the same
society, tugging in contrary ways. The systems under construction are
so complex that they are inaccessible to most people, and the speed of
change requires more than they may have in them to keep up. Yet the
Internet allows for a world-wide conversation, the most participatory
and democratic form of mass speech yet developed.

The simple Nicaraguan cross I used as an illustration in my
talk at the end of term assembly (it was Holy Week, and in Plockton

[1] Angus Peter Campbell, *Rote Learning*, in *One Road*, Fountain Publishing, Isle of Skye, 1994, p. 116.
[2] Jean de Munck, *The Ethical, Cultural and Democratic Stakes of the Information Society*, duplicated document, European Commission, 1996.

it was permitted to talk about Jesus) depicts a peasant crucified on a cross made from his own spade and pitchfork—'... the personal, the authentic and the local.'

*   *   *

The journey from Kyle of Lochalsh took me along Loch Carron, past the Achnashellach Forest, Achnasheen, Achanalt, and down by Garve and Contin to the fertile country bordering on the Black Isle. I was met in Dingwall by the minister's wife from Fearn and Nigg who had been stocking up on foodstuffs for her goats. When we arrived at the manse the dogs greeted me with loud barking and the cats with a close inspection. In the afternoon my host took me on a tour of the coastal villages of Portmahomack, Balnapaling, Balintore and the Royal Burgh of Tain. His precious eight-year-old grand-daughter, who came with us to walk the dogs and play on the stony beach at Nigg, opposite the wartime gun emplacements at the entrance to the firth, had been born with a hole in her heart.

It was to Fearn Abbey that, at the age of fourteen, a young Scottish nobleman named Patrick Hamilton was appointed absentee abbot. This honour paid for his education on the continent—in Paris where he graduated master of arts, in Louvain where he came under the influence of Erasmus and the new Humanism, and in Wittenberg where he was taught by Luther and Melanchthon. Returning to St Andrews, filled with an uncompromising evangelical zeal, he was not 25 years old in 1528 when they burnt him at the stake, the first Scottish martyr of the Reformation. Every Sunday morning as a student in St Andrews I walked past the spot where he died, his initials marked in the cobblestones outside the University Chapel.

Invergordon with its age-old haven in the Cromarty Firth offers reminders of past and present, war and peace. Great skeins of wild geese were constantly on the move, swaying overhead like the horizontal, hanging angel of Barlach's Güstrow war memorial. The oil industry has changed the face of the town as much as did the second world war. An aging German told me he had come to Invergordon as a prisoner of war and stayed ever since. He had seen all the changes.

At the north end of the town, drawn up above high water, was a sailing boat (I passed it several times)—old, clinker built, undecked, pointed at bow and stern—an east-coast fifie, beautifully repainted, somebody's pride and joy, waiting for the stepping of her mast and the launch of another summer's sailing in the firth and racing with the dolphins out at sea.

Next morning I was invited to speak to an ecumenical study group at St Joseph's Catholic church in Invergordon. We met informally over coffee in the church hall. In the middle of discussion, out of the blue, a woman asked me what living on the continent had meant for me and how it had affected my faith.

I don't remember exactly what I said to her, and other exchanges followed my reply. But afterwards the question wouldn't go away. What has it meant for me, all these years of rooting around Europe and the church? I turned the question over and over in my mind, until it became a kind of shorter catechism about places and meaning:

> Man's chief end is
> to make sense of the world,
> to cauterize despair,
> to make room for joy and celebration,
> to get ready to die.

*   *   *

That November evening in the Stavronikita Monastery on the Holy Mountain, my companions fast asleep after the long day's walk from Ouranopolis by way of Kariai, and I, wanting the moment to last, listening to the rhythm of their breathing and the faint accompaniment of waves breaking on the shore some seventy feet below. I had found the peace I sought at last. The dormitory was a wooden gallery high up under the roof, jutting out over the monastery's mediaeval walls and bulwarks on a cliff top on the east side of Mount Athos. A latticed window ran the length of the room overlooking the sea. It was simply furnished and heated by a sweetly smelling stove. An olive oil lamp stood in a pool of soft light on the plain, scrubbed table where I sat. As I looked out into the darkness in the direction of Samothrace, the Winged Victory appeared to my longing eyes, and I saw her, freed from the prison house of the Louvre, head high (oh the splendour of her long-lost face and hair), come striding through the air on outstretched wings—a fantastic vision of redemption, to complement the beauty

97

of the holy icon I adored at vespers in the candlelight and shadows of the catholicon.

*   *   *

Le Rouet is an abandoned hamlet in the Queyras, surrounded by thin alpine pastures on a ledge above the gorges of the Gil. At six thousand feet the view south over the valley looks to where the rocky mountains climb out of their clothing of forest, naked, austere, revealing. The great dilapidated school house at the entrance to the village once rang with children's voices. Its thick stone walls, plastered and painted on the inside, protected them against the winter's bitter cold. High up, a narrow balcony, which was the children's playground when the snow was deep, shelters under eves of *bardeaux*—the long larch tiles which still cover a roof whose carpenters could have built the Golden Hind. The date on the lintel above the stout door is 1789. In this building, architecture and reassurance are marvellously combined. Against its sturdy side our *bergerie*, the barn where we used to spend summer holidays, leans like a little sister.

The wind blowing down the valley of the Gil lifts my kite aloft so that its tail draws fanciful pictures in the sky. From its vantage point it can see the distant Ravin de Ruine Blanche, a cascade of white rocks where a soft stone gully collapsed centuries ago, the sharp Pointe de la Selle, the Saddle, and Ceillac, village of the mystical name. The highest mountain there, by the Lac St Anne with its lone chapel, is the Pic de la Fonte Sancte, where the pure snow of winter renews the baptismal waters of the earth each year. One night I dreamt I was the kite, soaring in pure delight upon the wind, gazing down at my old self, tugging at the umbilical cord of my new birth.

*   *   *

Catarina Jagellonica Regina Sueciae,
Johannes III Rex Sueciae, his queen,
Polish princess from distant Cracow,
who died in 1583, and is buried between
St Erik and Archbishop Nathan Söderblom
in Uppsala Cathedral (her death came
mid-way in time between). Her epitaph

written on the stained-glass aureole of a tall
window in the austere church reads:
NEMO NISI MORS: 'No one
but death' will divide us.

*   *   *

Storks wheeling in the evening air, one here, one there, others to right
and left along the foothills of the Guadarrama Mountains, below the
esplanade of the Escorial. There the Castilian plain begins—the barren
Castilian plateau, Unamuno's 'horizontal Christ' which he compared
to the lifeless body of the Saviour (it stretches away south past Madrid).
Space circumscribed, and time contained, the circle holds in the grand
slow motion of the birds' wide gyre: the unobtrusive demonstration
of the unremitting animation of the earth.

*   *   *

When after two years you returned to Solentiname, Juan,
            a child of five then,
I remember perfectly what you said to me:
'You're the one that's going to tell me all about God,
            right?'
And I increasingly
            have come to know less of God.
A mystic, that is, a lover of God
            called him NOTHING,
and another said: whatever you say about him is false.
And the best way for you to have knowledge of God
was perhaps for me not to be talking to you about God.[3]

*   *   *

On a flight from Costa Rica's San José to Guatemala City in the eighties,
out of a porthole of the aeroplane I looked down on the turquoise
waters of Lake Nicaragua and caught a glimpse of the thickly wooded

---

[3] Ernesto Cardenal, *Cosmic Canticle,* Canto 18, *Flights of Victory,* Curbstone, Willimantic,
CT, 1993, p. 160.

archipelago of Solentiname. History had added to the beauty of the view, for by then Ernesto Cardenal was Nicaragua's Minister of Culture. In the years before the Sandinista Revolution, it was there in Solentiname that he nourished his faith in a community of peasants and fisherfolk far from the *hauts lieux* of socialist ideology and liberation theology.

I flew home to Brussels over a calm North Sea on a glorious day at the beginning of spring. A hazy azure sky mixed indistinctly at the horizon with the opalescent grey-blue sea. The lumps and scratches on its surface were ships set on their courses, and here and there a clutch of what looked like little boxes turned out to be oil platforms, inconspicuous in the immensity of the ocean—tiny and vulnerable, incongruous, compared to their gigantic bulk in the yards and dry docks of Nigg and Invergordon.

This horizon I call home

A delicate new moon attended by Venus in the still, black, early Sunday morning sky, saw me off by taxi from Morningside. The November storms of the last few days were finally over, the buffeting winds I had contended with at the corners of Edinburgh's streets and closes. Waverley, when I arrived, was sleepy-eyed. Few other passengers were about as I boarded the train for Perth. As it crept through the massive structure of the Forth Bridge, lights, twinkling in the shadows of the tankers and tugs anchored in the waters of the oil port below, transmitted the bewitching lure of heavy industry before the day's work begins.

Inverkeithing, Aberdour, Burntisland, Kinghorn, Kirkcaldy: the train followed the coastal towns of Fife's underbelly as dawn came up on the islands of Inchcolm and Inchkeith and, across the wide firth, the Salisbury Crags and Arthur's Seat. Branching inland east of the Lomond Hills the railway crosses the fertile Vale of Eden and climbs the Ochils behind Strathmiglo and Auchtermuchty before descending by Glen Farg on the other side. I knew this country as a boy.

Hoar frost on the fields. A white and patient pony stood to watch the early train go by. Wisps of cloud were clearing from the hilltops to make way for a weak sun. I too was waking up. The view south from the Ochil Hills takes in the full extent of the Lomonds, their uncomplicated sky-line dominating the perspective uninterruptedly from east to west. A gentle gradient swells from Markinch and Ladybank up to the steep rise which gives East Lomond its summit above Falkland Palace. Then there's a sweep of moorland joining the two peaks, broken only by a wooded cleft where the road winds up and over in the middle. West Lomond's volcanic cone completes the range, which falls immediately away over an escarpment, down to the low lying land around Loch Leven. The profile of the hills is archetypal, like the shoulders of a compassionate colossus of the north helping a weary Atlas to hold up the heavens, like a woman's breasts thrusting against the yielding body of the sky. There is comfort and reassurance here. This horizon I call home.

*

When we went to live in Roubaix, I never thought I'd come to love the plains of northern France and Belgium, *avec des cathédrales pour uniques montagnes ...,* as Jacques Brel puts it. We had a friend called Renée who was a doctor in Lille, an anarchist at heart. Her family home was in the village of Etricourt in Picardy. Whatever the season, whatever the weather, much of it was a melancholy ride from Roubaix to Etricourt, because of the war cemeteries along the way. Once there, however, it was like coming home. Renée had that French delight in food and drink however elaborate or simple. A walnut tree grew in the garden of her house. In summertime she'd make a walnut wine aperitif from the green fleshy pods and nuts sliced through and left to soak in red wine and alcohol. And at All Saints, when the leaves were falling, I'd climb the tree to pluck the last nuts from the branches and our three- or four-year-old would help me gather the harvest into baskets to be stored in the cellar for salads and desserts throughout the year.

*

Between the Ponte San Angelo and the Piazza Navona in Rome there's a neighbourhood of narrow streets and solid tenements with little workshops tucked away in the vaults and arches of the walls. It represents an immemorial domestic culture of tradesmen and artisans— locksmiths, joiners, wicker workers, cabinetmakers, plumbers, cobblers, tailors, bakers—the other side of the sophisticated society of Rome, the rich élite, the church. In their purpose and proportion they convey a sense of well-being, a way to be at home. The past is present, life's pace is meaningful, and people have the time to be.

*

I've heard the sound of the wind blowing in the ancient oaks of Västerås which spill their acorns in profusion in September by the lake. Oaks have grown here for fifteen thousand years. In the forests of Västerås Sweden's iron age began, and Nordic Europeans first discovered how to smelt iron and forge it into iron tools. Though the wind in autumn in the great oaks of Västerås is not so different from the wind at other times in other trees in other places, to me the sound of it there was special. Nowhere else will it ever be the same.

*

I wrote a simple poem years ago which had a missing word. For all the dictionaries I consulted and the thesauruses I searched, I never found it. It remained beyond my reach.

> [. . .] returns to me, gentle, still
> like gulls flying home over evening hills
> to make their peace with the storm-weary sea

Maybe it was hidden in a recess of my mind, or lost, or never was. As if its meaning were a secret too deep to share.

> 'Somewhere' there must be a point where the criterion of truth does not lie with me; 'somewhere' ... there will be a point where it will not be a matter of agreement between my thinking and what has been thought ... 'Somewhere' man must definitely submit; he must let himself be told that he is not autonomous, that he cannot be either a creator or a judge of the universe. 'Somewhere' he will have to grasp, not so much in ecstasy as in sober apprehension of the truth, the privilege of understanding that he is understood and known and chosen.[1]

Low tide and mud flats on the upper reaches of the firth of Tay, some startled wildfowl in the reeds, an ancient oak-tree lying at the edge of a field, its great trunk shattered by the recent storms. Then suddenly, with a rush of noise, into the tunnel that takes the train through the escarpment and down to the fair city. A grey heron gracefully, deliberately, circles the roofs of the prison.

*   *   *

It was Remembrance Sunday in a farming village north of Perth. As

---

[1] Kornelis H Miskotte, *When the Gods are Silent*, Collins, London, 1967, p. 15.

I walked up the hill towards the church following a brief ceremony at the war memorial I noticed a sticker on a member of the congregation's car: 'Stuff the EU. Eat Scottish beef!' It brought home to me how complex preaching to the establishment may be. The British lack of self-critique in the international arena owes so much to our island status, to the global dominance of the English language, to the fact that, unlike most other European nations, we were not humiliated one way or another in the last world war (through defeat, occupation or collaboration). How do you speak from a pulpit in rural Perthshire about federalism, the Brussels bureaucracy, or at best a distant democratic process, on Remembrance Day?

The minister of Kenmore drove me to Rannoch, up from Loch Tay and over the shoulder of Schiehallion, down to Kinloch Rannoch, whence following the south side of the loch to Rannoch School, where I was to speak. Long ago I went by Land Rover on a winter journey across a bleak and snowy Rannoch Moor as far as where the road ends. Ever since, the place has seemed to me to be a mystery. Rannoch is at the heart of Scotland, geographically the very core of the mainland, yet the road ends here in moor and bog and wilderness. The traveller who would go on must take to footpaths and sheep tracks, precarious at the best of times and dangerous in winter, for here civilisation reaches the end of its tether.

I wished I were walking on the open road.

*   *   *

After the visit to the school my host drove me back by way of Loch Tummel and the Queen's View where we stopped to look at the last of the autumn colours in the trees, and admire Schiehallion in the distance with its soft powdering of snow.

> ... Schiehallion in my mind
> Is more than mountain.
> In it he [landscape] leaves behind
> A meaning, an idea ...[2]

---

[2] Norman MacCaig, *Landscape and I* in *Collected Poems*, Chatto & Windus, London, 1985, p. 294.

It was on the rocks and heather of this beautiful mountain that the ashes of one of the greatest Scottish painters of the twentieth century, John Duncan Fergusson, were scattered thirty-five years ago.

Schiehallion provides a less obvious memorial to J D Fergusson than the exquisite Round House by the River Tay in Perth. Built in 1832 for the city's Water Works, it now houses the Fergusson Gallery which surely is the most happily arranged and satisfying small art gallery imaginable. The exhibition I visited was a joint one including works by JD Fergusson and his friend S J Peploe, hung together. Similarities and differences in their work were represented by paintings from Scotland, France and England, arranged according to period. It began with Fergusson's small early painting of *Princes Street Gardens, Edinburgh*. His female nudes, like the bold *Torse de Femme* were not on show, I suppose, because they have no counterpart in Peploe's oeuvre. *Margaret Morris dans le 'Chant Hindu'*, which may appear to some as arrogant and overbearing, is a good indication of Fergusson's sense of freedom. Stand back, it seems to say, whar daur meddle wi' me! He drew inspiration for his painting from the Declaration of Arbroath.

In *Modern Scottish Painting*, the introduction to painting which he wrote in his middle sixties for young Scottish artists, he writes:

> At the risk of being considered anti-English, which I'm not, here is the Arbroath Manifesto. Put the same thing into painting and you've got what I'd call Scottish painting…
> *'It is not glory, it is not riches, neither is it honour, but it is liberty alone that we fight and contend for, which no honest man will lose but with his life!'*[3]

Painting for Fergusson (1874-1961) was not just a craft or profession but 'a sustained attempt at finding a means of expressing reactions to life in the form demanded by each new experience'. From his early impatience at medical college and art schools in Edinburgh which led him to abandon formal education and teach himself to paint 'in nature's school', to *Modern Scottish Painting*, Fergusson was a radical in his approach to art and life. He was a friend of Picasso and the Fauves—Matisse, Derain, Vlaminck—and exhibited regularly with them in Paris. At the same time he cherished his links with Peploe,

---

[3] J D Fergusson, *Modern Scottish Painting*, William Mackellan, Glasgow, 1943, p. 24.

Cadell and Hunter, the other Scottish Colourists. In the Paris of the decade before the First World War, Diaghilev, Nijinsky, Stravinsky and the Ballet Russe influenced his art—and Margaret Morris, the dancer he met in France and fell in love with. Her ashes are scattered on Schiehallion too.

France was essential for Fergusson's development as an artist. Scotland was his cultural home, but Paris provided a necessary counterpart. At the beginning of the twentieth century Paris was unique in the world of art, and Fergusson's genius was that he grasped this early on. 'Something new had started ... But there was no language for it that made sense in Edinburgh or London ...' Its influence on him is a lesson in creative encounter with a foreign culture. Without it his radical ideas for the direction of Scottish art would never have matured. 'If Scotland ... would make a "new alliance" with France,' he wrote in *Modern Scottish Painting,* 'not *political* like the "auld alliance", but *cultural,* it would perhaps put Scotland back on to the main track of her culture ... Paris is simply a place of freedom ... It allowed me to be Scots as I understand it ...'[4]

In the years leading up to the Commune of 1871, the last of the nineteenth century European revolutions, Richard Wagner was in Paris writing the libretto for *The Mastersingers of Nuremberg.* It wasn't many years before Fergusson went to live there. *Die Meistersinger* portrays the struggle between the new and the old in art: how a young French knight, Walther von Stoltzing, who had learned to sing in nature's school, had to struggle to be accepted by the German burghers' guilds. With the help of the master cobbler, Hans Sachs, his song was refashioned in such a way as to enchant the people of Nuremberg and at the same time transform the very rules of the conservative mastersingers' art. Sachs is the epitome of European culture's striving for freedom, and—who knows?—it's as if J D Fergusson, in what he sought to do for twentieth century Scottish painting, took Hans Sachs as his model!

---

[4] *Op. cit.,* pp. 69,70.

You can't be a Scotsman all your life

Gloomy November, the stubble fields of faded green and gold are the resting place of the wild goose which rises from the sodden earth to wheel away as the bus rumbles down the road from Fraserburgh to Peterhead. At this time of year the sun reaches only ten or twelve degrees above the horizon. With rain like today and such low cloud it'll not get light all day. I was staying at the manse of Crimond, where the clock on the old church tower has sixty-one minutes to the hour, and the 23rd Psalm tune bears witness against the pace and pain of modern life. The bus passes St Fergus with its enormous, brightly lit, industrial processing plant for North Sea gas, which has caught up on this ancient homeland of the Picts. The north-east corner of Scotland has little to commend it in winter, apart from the birds which stop here in their thousands to rest and feed.

The origin of the name Peterhead is not known for sure. A church dedicated to St Peter once stood by the river Ugie north of the town, and some say the original name evolved from Inverugie Petri to Peterugie to Peterhead. More likely the name comes from the ancient Pictish, Pettayruisge—homestead (*pett*), by (*ayr*), the water (*uisge*)—later to be associated with the church of St Peter, built on this headland of rock jutting out into the North Sea, the most easterly point of Scotland.

The Ugie Fish House still smokes local salmon and sea trout, netted off shore in the summer months. Winter brings imports from Orkney fish farms. Solidly built of pink granite, with tiny windows and stepped gables, the smoke house stands by itself near a ruddy golden beach at the mouth of the Ugie. It is the oldest building in Peterhead, dating from 1585. In the dark low-ceilinged shop a kindly fishwife apologized to me that EC regulations no longer allowed her to show me round. But she described the work she and her husband and two cousins do to maintain their flourishing trade. And as a matter of course she asked after the health of the minister I was staying with, following his recent operation. 'We've been praying for him at church,' she said.

The fish market, the fishermen's mission, and the industrial workshops crowding the harbour are all part of a larger culture one might see in different forms in the streets of any working Scottish town. But Peterhead has the trappings of great wealth as well. Skippers and boat-owners sport Alpha Romeo coupés and BMW saloons. There is an abundance of electronic consumer goods in the shops and the window of the bakery in Broad Street is piled with three-storey wedding cakes for the conspicuous wedding parties of rich fishermen's daughters.

In Peterhead museum there's a painting of the town by a Mary Forbes, daughter of John Forbes, himself a portrait painter. Her 'View of Peterhead' is a delightful nineteenth century oval canvas of the Fishertoon seen from the south across the wide expanse of the harbour-bay. Fishermen busy on a boat with its sails furled occupy the foreground, and beneath a light blue sky with clouds, the houses, churches, harbour and inch of Peterhead line the farther shore (the prison wasn't built). Mary Forbes exhibited at the Royal Scottish Academy in 1851 and 1854. A pity she then emigrated to America. There is a brightness and colour in her work which is quite absent from the other paintings in the gallery.

The museum tells the story of Peterhead from its foundation in 1593 by the 5th Earl Marischal, George Keith, whose family castle lies in ruins in Inverugie. Peterhead's fishing past is displayed with artifacts, model boats and pictures from the days of open long-boats and square-rigged yawls, through the years of whaling when men wintered on the arctic ice, to the boom times of the herring drifters with their tall smokestacks and tiny mizzen sails. Today the town boasts the largest white fish port in northern Europe.

The worst gales come from the south-east and that's where this gale was coming from. Huge waves pounded the breakwater or surged mountainous past the harbour mouth. The port was crowded with fishing boats sheltering from the storm, stocky metal shells equipped with the latest nets and winches, sonar and satellite technology—the combine harvesters of the sea. Peterhead's conflicts with the European Commission regarding methods and quotas underline the uneasy stand-off between technical developments in the fishing industry and the sea it takes for granted. This is hardly fishing. This is industrial spoiling of the seas: a combination of greed, technocracy, and either culpable ignorance or carelessness. It can have no long-term future. It offers no assurance. It is to fishing what agribusiness is to farming.

Only the names of the fishing boats belie their tough, uncompromising exterior: *Providence, Devotion, Mystic, Elegance, Celestial Dawn, Rose of Sharon, El Shaddai* (God with us). As though for all their modernisation, for all the efforts of technology and risk management to transform the fisherman's lot, there remains the suspicion, the superstition, that he's no match for the overarching power of the elements. The day after I had lunch with the ministers' fraternal in Ellon, a helicopter winch man from that small town was swept into the sea and drowned while rescuing the crew from a shipwreck off Shetland. And all the time I was in the north-east a huge barge crane from Rotterdam was sheltering behind the South Pier, waiting for calm weather to attempt the salvage of the *Sapphire*, a boat which went down eight weeks earlier with four men aboard. Death at sea is what links the present to Peterhead's past perhaps more than anything else. It makes, so they say, for a proneness to religion in the coastal towns and villages of Buchan. Inland, the farming folk are 'no sae kirk greedy'.

The Old Pretender, afraid of interception by English east coast naval patrols on his way from France to Peterhead in 1715, took the sea route up the west side of Britain. Hugging the coast he sailed through the Irish Sea to the Sea of the Hebrides, up the Minch, around Cape Wrath, the 'point of turning', over to Duncansby Head by way of the Pentland Firth, across the wide Moray Firth to Kinnaird Head, and so down to Peterhead.

Kinnaird Head was always a clear landmark for navigators. It was mentioned as early as 140 AD by Ptolemy, the geographer of Alexandria. For centuries sailors used it as a point from which to take a bearing eastwards across the North Sea to the continent. When it was visible, that is. The first lighthouse in Scotland was built there in 1787 on top of the sixteenth century keep of the Fraser family, founders of Fraserburgh. The British government created the Scottish Lighthouse Commission following a terrible winter of storms and shipwrecks on Scotland's coasts in 1782. The original light came from a clutch of whale oil lamps reflected in mirrors and replenished by keepers throughout the night. It could be seen for miles out to sea.

In the brilliance of a sunny November day my view from the Kinnaird Head lighthouse was spectacular. The remains of three weeks of storms brought row after row of huge brown, sandy waves surging in on the beach that stretches westwards from the headland, crashing and tumbling in a mist of spume. The force of the ocean's swell, what remained of the storm, was awesome. As I walked along the cliff path below the castle, I felt the shock of the waves pounding the solid rock beneath my feet.

*   *   *

Outside Peterhead's Town House at the top of Broad Street is an imposing bronze statue of an eighteenth century figure in a wig and frock coat, right hand outstretched and holding a scroll: a member of the nobility, an ambassador perhaps, a man at ease with the great and the good. It is a statue of James Keith, younger brother of George, the Tenth Earl Marischal of Inverugie. George and James Keith were Jacobites, supporters of the Old Pretender. On 23 September 1715, by order of the Earl Marischal, James (the son of James II who fled England in 1688) was proclaimed King at the Market Cross of Peterhead to replace the 'wee, wee German Lairdie', George I. Three months later, on 22 December, he landed with a few attendants at Port Henry Pier in Peterhead in heavy rain to begin his uninspiring bid to retrieve the fortunes of the Stewart house. He failed miserably and was soon surreptitiously sailing from Montrose to France again, leaving behind him an unsettled reckoning. George Keith, the Earl Marischal, his life forfeit, fled the country. His estates were confiscated. His brother James went into exile too.

The monument in Broad Street is the replica of a marble statue of James Keith which was erected in Berlin's Wilhelm Platz after his death. It was presented to the town in 1869 by William I of Prussia. Keith is described in an old history book I found in the Peterhead library as 'the glory of the Buchan district ... probably the most renowned man it has produced.' And thereby hangs a tale.

In eighteenth century Europe, there was a different kind of free movement of persons, goods and services from what the European Union makes possible today. But it existed nonetheless. Its common currency was still to a certain extent religion, but more so war. Princedoms and nation states had taken over from the church as the organising principle of the continent, just as economics holds it now. After the failure of the uprising in 1715, many Highlanders went off to fight in the French or Spanish armies, for the sake of employment. Some used it as a training for the Forty-five. James Keith followed suit, serving for several years as an officer in the Spanish army and, in 1726-7, taking part in one of the Spanish sieges of Gibraltar. During this time he and his brother were involved in another failed attempt at a Stewart uprising in Scotland, with Spanish support. The expedition landed in Lewis in 1719, but was so insignificant it is hardly ever mentioned alongside the Fifteen and the Forty-five. On his escape route Keith managed a visit home, and boarded a ship in Peterhead for Texel in the Netherlands.

James Keith was no Catholic, coming from the episcopalian stronghold of the north-east, and this worked against him in Spain. In 1728 he accepted a commission in the Russian army as Major-General, distinguishing himself first in the War of the Polish Succession in 1733-35, then as commander of the Russian forces in the Ukraine, and subsequently in a campaign against the Ottoman Turks which ended in 1737. He was rewarded with the Governorship of the Ukraine, before being dispatched again to command Russian forces in the war with Sweden in 1741-3. On the conclusion of peace with Sweden, the country calling for assistance from Russia in view of a conflict with Denmark, Keith was dispatched to Stockholm in the double capacity of Commander-in-Chief of the Russian forces and Ambassador Plenipotentiary for the Empress Elizabeth the Great at the Swedish Court.

In 1747 he left the Russian service and joined his brother in the court of Frederick the Great of Prussia, who made him a Field-Marshal in the Prussian army and Governor of Berlin. A fine military portrait of Field-Marshall James Keith by Antoine Pesne, dating from this period, hangs in the Scottish National Portrait Gallery in Edinburgh. With the outbreak of the Seven Years War, the last major European conflict before the French Revolution involving all the great powers, Keith played a leading role in campaigns in Saxony and Bohemia and in the defence of Prussia. He died at the battle of Hochkirch in Saxony in 1758 at the age of 62. His epitaph reads, 'While in battle not far from here he was restoring by courage, gesture, call and example, the wavering line of his soldiers, he fell fighting like a hero.'

An old Dictionary of National Biography describes Keith as 'by far the greatest of all soldier Scots abroad'. He would probably have agreed with Kenneth White's: 'Shit, you can't be a Scotsman *all* your life ... You've got to get out there and mix it more. *Make* something of it.'[1] Was the culture of nobility and war enough to ensure his integration in European society? In what languages did he give orders to his officers and men? Who were his friends? Did his ways cross the path of the Young Pretender as he wandered dissolutely across Europe after the defeat of the Forty-five?

Keith never married, but while living in Sweden he fell in love with a young orphan Eva Merthens, whom he adopted and who bore him children. She outlived him by over fifty years. Thomas Carlyle added these words to his epitaph—'Keith sleeps now ... far from bonny Inverugie: the hoarse sea-winds and caverns of Dunnottar singing vague requiems to his honourable line and him ...'

---

[1] Kenneth White, *The Blue Road*, Mainstream, Edinburgh, 1990, p. 16.

East Lothian
The little place

'Moon and sun are travellers of eternity, and the years coming and going are wanderers too. Drifting life away on a boat, or meeting age leading a horse by the mouth, each day is a journey and the journey itself is home. Many of the men of old died upon the journey. I too for years past have been drawn by the sight of a blown cloud to ceaseless thoughts of roaming.'[1] Bashō's last travel record, *The Narrow Road to the Deep North,* which begins with these words, has been called a 'study in eternity', a 'monument ... against the flow of time'.

It's a short walk inland from Dunbar to Spott, especially on a spring morning like this with dazzling clouds and the first skylark of the year singing irrepressibly. Shading my eyes against the light I searched the sky for it, in vain. But it's the lark's song rather than its brown, crested, hovering form, that fires the imagination. I was glad to hear it: agricultural methods have caused skylarks to decline in Western Europe by as much as three-quarters in recent years. Today the song accompanied me on my way, and was relayed by others along the road.

> Skylark sings all
> day, and day
> not long enough.[2]

Bashō was composing haiku in seventeenth century Japan at the time when the Wars of the Covenant were rending Scotland apart.

> Skylark on moor—
> sweet song
> of non-attachment.[3]

---

[1] Cf. Matsuo Bashō, *The Narrow Road to Oku,* trans. Donald Keene, Kodansha International, London, 1996; Matsuo Bashō, *The Narrow Road to the Deep North and other travel sketches,* trans. Nobuyuki Yuasa, Penguin, London, 1966; Matsuo Bashō, *Back Roads to Far Towns,* trans. Cid Corman and Kamaike Susumu, The Ecco Press, Hopewell, New Jersey, 1968.

[2] Lucien Stryk, *Bashō: On Love and Barley,* Penguin, London, 1985, p. 51.

[3] *Op. cit.,* p. 42.

Lightness of touch, the poetic quality with which Bashō joins the two parts of the haiku, also supplies the link between the world of nature and the transcendent.[4] In his tiny poems the temporal and the eternal, the microcosm and the order of the cosmos are joined as in a sacrament. First comes the experience—here we have a skylark singing, all day, or on the moor; then after the break the sudden contrasting awareness—the day's brief span or the detachment which results from being one with nature.

The road to Spott winds past fields belonging to a farm called Little Pinkerton, where in 1650 the Battle of Dunbar was fought between the Covenanters under General David Leslie and Oliver Cromwell's English army. The Scots were an 'army of clerks and ministers' sons', as one disgruntled officer styled them, purged of professional soldiers by religious bigots who regarded them as ungodly and unworthy. Leslie, though he was an experienced commander who had served the King of Sweden in the Thirty Years War, allowed himself to be persuaded by zealous Covenanters to abandon his commanding position on Doon Hill, the vantage point which dominates this north east corner of the Lothians, and confront Cromwell's smaller army on the narrow coastal plain below. It was a strategic blunder that cost him the death of 3,000 men and more than three times as many prisoners.

Crossed swords on the map also mark the place two miles away where three and a half centuries earlier, in 1296, during the Scottish Wars of Independence, John Balliol's forces were defeated by Edward I at another Battle of Dunbar. As if the rich brown earth, moist and newly ploughed for sowing, were testifying that these fields around me had been wet with the blood of two terrible Scottish disasters.

Spott is not far away, on the slopes of Brunt Hill. It remains true to its name, in Old Norse 'the little place'. A nearby spring, St John's Well, was a stopping place on the ancient pilgrim route from Iona to Lindisfarne, and may have been the reason why it was first settled. In the thirteenth century Knights Templar from Coldingham Priory held much of the land round about and made use of the kirk. And some of the stonework of today's church dates from that time. By the end of the fifteenth century an out-station of the Church of

---

[4] *Op. cit.*, p. 10.

Dunbar was being built at Spott. Two centuries ago its population reached a peak of 612. Today there are about 200 residents. At some expense and with outside help, they have come together to renovate the old red sandstone schoolhouse which, since its closure as a school after the Second World War, has served as a beautiful village hall and community centre.

The churchyard of Spott Kirk has four ancient elm-trees and several tall, straight pines within its walls. In 1881 a great storm blew down hundreds of trees in the area, some of which might otherwise still be there today. A copse behind what was the manse, across a field, is full of jackdaws, cackling like juvenile crows in the wind. The elm outside the church door grows on ground where some of Cromwell's soldiers were buried after the battle. The tools of various trades essential to a village of the time—smiths, masons, carpenters and weavers—are sculpted on some of the eighteenth century tombstones. The pathos of infant mortality in an age before medical science transformed life expectancy is obvious from one of the nineteenth century tombstones:

ERECTED
BY
ROBERT ANGUS. IN MEMORY
OF HIS DAUGHTER HELLEN
WHO DIED IN INFANCY.
AND MARY. WHO DIED 2ND AUGT.
1836 AGED 2 YEARS.
ALSO HIS SON ROBERT WHO
DIED 21ST SEP. 1838 AGED 2 YEARS
AND HELLEN ALISON ANGUS
SPOUSE TO WILLIAM ANDERSON
WHO DIED AT GLOSTERSHIRE 10TH JUNE
1854 AGED 25 YEARS.

It was Mothering Sunday and the little kirk was full of flowers, to be distributed later by members of the congregation to the old and sick of the parish. My host had been minister of Belhaven and Spott for twenty years. The mother of the baby he baptised that day was once a child in his Sunday School.

After Sunday lunch we talked about the ministry—births, marriages and deaths, especially deaths. He reckoned he had seen just

115

about everything in his time: a woman crossing the ford of a river in spate which washed her car away and drowned her child, the young foolhardy fisherman drowned at sea leaving a young family, farm accidents, a murder in the High Street, the son of members of the congregation killed in an air crash on the other side of the world, 'the Dunbar cancer cluster'—the high incidence of cancer, inexplicable but for the Torness nuclear power station nearby.

* * *

An elegant antique cast iron signpost at the road junction in Spott indicates the direction and the precise distance southwards to BRUNT 1¾, WOODHALL 2 ⅞, and ELMSCLEUGH 3¼. As I toiled uphill to the Brunt, a cock pheasant gave me the momentary benefit of its doubt by cocking a scarlet cheek at me, before it rushed off across a field with a whirring cry.

From the summit the view south takes in the escarpment of Lothian Edge and the Lammermuirs beyond. Northwards it includes the various rocky outcrops of the region on land and sea from Traproin, North Berwick Law and the Bass Rock to the shipshape Isle of May which guards the entrance to the Firth of Forth. The eye follows the coastline from Dunbar with its two churches and ruined hotel, past the golf course to Belhaven beach sweeping north west to where the little river Tyne flows swiftly into the sea. Beyond it is a headland with a rock formation called St Baldred's Cradle, and then more beach, the Ravensheugh Sands, which stretch for two miles till rocks again flank the channel separating the coast from the Bass Rock. In the other direction the Torness power station is out of sight.

Much of this coastal area is now a nature reserve named after John Muir, the native of Dunbar who emigrated to the USA as a child in 1849, and became one of America's greatest naturalists and the founder of her national parks. 'I asked the boulders I met whence they came and whither they were going,' he wrote about his childhood and youth. 'Around my native town of Dunbar, I loved ... best of all to watch the waves in awful storms thundering on the black headlands and craggy ruins of the old Dunbar Castle, where the sea and the sky, the waves and the clouds were mingled together as one ...'

Someone on the radio that morning had been talking about the search to develop a technology which 'eradicates failure'. Evidence of results of the struggle to master nature and the human condition was all around me—from the impact of agricultural methods on the skylark, the carnage of war, and infant mortality to cancer clusters. I suppose it is only when, encouraged by a certain level of success, our civilisation makes a god out of technology, that the concept of eradicating failure could even arise.

One glorious day in May ten years ago, I was walking on the Ravensheugh Sands with Professor Raimon Panikkar, disciple and teacher barefoot together. It was his day off from the centenary Gifford Lectures. We had had lunch in Haddington, left the car at the road end beyond Tynninghame, and followed the timeless path through the tall pine trees to the dunes and the beach. Few other people were about. Gannets from the Bass Rock were fishing by companies all down the coast, circling over shoals of fish, and diving relentlessly into the sea. No wonder the French call them *les fous de Bassan*—the crazy ones from the Bass Rock, their madness being in the way they dive.

Professor Panikkar was explaining to me what he was later to call the Tragic Law of Technocratic Society: 'whatever progress there is in the micro-social order represents a regression in the macro-social order ... Once we have broken the natural rhythms, balance—indeed justice—towards nature is no longer possible.'[5] A simple example can be made of the motor car, which, in its early years was a great step forward in micro-social terms—offering individuals freedom of movement, transport, recreation. But a limit has now been reached and passed. On the macro-social level there are far too many motor cars, with all the negative effect that that implies for nature and the environment. Panikkar's law is rooted in the rhythm of nature and follows the classical logic of tragedy. Here, it demonstrates, we are not just in the realm of ethics, but of something much greater, involving human destiny.

> Over skylark's song
> *Noh* cry
> of pheasant[6]

For Bashō the pheasant's call had the pathos of the cries of grief heard in *Noh* theatre.

---

[5]   *1492-1992 Conquète et évangile en amérique latine: Questions pour l'Europe aujourd'hui*, p. 39.

[6]   Lucien Stryk, *op. cit.*, p. 30.

Come, see real
flowers
of this painful world.[7]

'When we try to pick out anything by itself,' John Muir wrote shortly before his death, 'we find it hitched to everything else in the universe.' On the crumbling walls of Dunbar Castle which once welcomed Mary Queen of Scots, and which Cromwell demolished, the din of hundreds of nesting gulls is overwhelming.

---

7 *Ibid.*, p. 54.

Gateway of the giants

Olaf the Peacock was the son of Hoskuld Dala-Kollsson and a slave-girl whom he bought for three marks of silver at a fair in Norway. Hoskuld was an Icelandic chieftain. His great-grandmother, Unn the Deep-Minded, was one of the early Norse pioneers who settled in Iceland in the last quarter of the ninth century when its only other inhabitants were Celtic anchorites in search of solitude. Unn's father, Ketil Flat-Nose, was a nobleman who chose to emigrate rather than forfeit his independence as King Harald Fine-Hair consolidated his feudal power in Norway.

Ketil went to Scotland because, as the *Laxdæla Saga* puts it, 'it was good living there. He knew the country well, for he had raided there extensively.'[1] He was well received and settled in the Hebrides. His daughter Unn grew into a respected matriarch who established dynasties in Scotland, Orkney and the Faeroe Islands by marrying off her grand-daughters to carefully chosen suitors. She settled finally in the virgin territory of Breidafjord on the north-west coast of Iceland. She and her brother, Bjorn the Easterner, became the progenitors of the families whose chronicle makes up the *Laxdæla Saga*. It sweeps through eight generations of a vibrant civilisation that dominated northern Europe including parts of Scotland at the end of the first millennium.

Hoskuld's concubine was called Melkorka. She was beautiful, but as the Russian who sold her to him said, she was mute. The night he bought her, he lay with her and she conceived. He took her home to Iceland in a long ship with a cargo of timber and rich gifts from King Harald. But after his return he left her alone. She turned out to be a woman of character and breeding. That winter she gave birth to a son whom Hoskuld called Olaf, 'a peerless child' whom he dearly loved.

One day Hoskuld surprised Melkorka and the child in conversation. Her dumbness had been a ploy. When questioned by

---

[1] *Laxdæla Saga*, translated with an introduction by Magnus Magnusson and Hermann Pálsson, Penguin, London, 1969, p. 49.

him, she revealed that her father was Myrkjartan, a king of Ireland. She had been taken captive and enslaved when she was fifteen.

When he was seven, Olaf was handed over to a foster father as was the custom in Iceland. He grew tall and strong, and was the most handsome man people had ever set eyes on; he always wore the finest clothing and weapons. Hoskuld called him 'the Peacock'.[2] Melkorka taught him to speak Irish and, when he was old enough, persuaded him, against his father's will, to visit Ireland. On his departure she gave him a fine gold ring her father Myrkjartan had given her as a teething gift: 'I expect he will recognise it when he sees it,' she said. She also gave him a knife and belt which her nurse had given her as a child.

Armed with these tokens, Olaf took ship for Norway where he wintered with King Harald. But he yearned to be on the move, and by summer, having attracted the patronage of the queen, he set off again by sea with sixty warriors. Not without difficulty, they reached Ireland, where their reception was hostile. Olaf was still only eighteen years of age.

The Irish wished to impound the ship offshore, but he argued with them in their own language and impressed them with his splendid appearance and the power of his fighting force. 'Olaf told his men to get their weapons out and line the gunwales of the ship from stem to stern. They stood so close that their shields overlapped all round the ship, with a spear-head jutting out from below every rim. Olaf walked forward to the prow. He was wearing a coat of mail, and had a gilded helmet on his head. He was girded with a sword whose pommel and guard were embossed with gold, and in his hand he held a barbed spear, chased and beautifully engraved. Before him he carried a red shield on which a lion was traced in gold.'[3] The Irishmen drew back and sent word hurriedly to the king.

King Myrkjartan arrives and in an exchange that echoes Jacob's meeting with Joseph in Egypt and Odysseus' reunion with Telemachus, the king allows himself to be convinced that the young man before him is his grandson. He invites Olaf and his men to join him at court, and they ride to Dublin. Melkorka's nurse who is by now bedridden, stricken with grief and old age, takes on a new lease of life at seeing Olaf and hearing the news that his mother, her foster-child, is alive and well in Iceland.

---

[2] *Op. cit.*, p. 77.
[3] *Op. cit.*, p. 91.

At that time there was constant warfare in the British Isles and Olaf the Peacock and his Norsemen served the king for a while as a fighting force. Myrkjartan is so impressed by his grandson's prowess and accomplishments that he offers him his kingdom after his death. But Olaf refuses and soon takes ship again for Norway. There, after another winter at King Harald's court, he sets sail for Iceland in a large merchant vessel loaded with timber, a gift from the king. Making land in Hrutafjord, he is met by his father, and rides home to Hoskuldstead. Soon Melkorka comes to see her son. She is only grieved that her old nurse has not been able to accompany him. Once the news gets round about Olaf's voyage and the esteem for him in Norway and Ireland, he becomes renowned in Iceland too. Though he is the son of a concubine he is considered the noblest of all of Hoskuld's sons. He marries and establishes a family and a grand estate in Laxriverdale.

The story of Olaf the Peacock, though it ranges back and forth across the North Atlantic, from Norway to Scotland, Iceland to Ireland, with its own particular blend of harsh nature and rough culture, occupies less than a third of the *Laxdæla Saga*. With the birth of two boys, Olaf's son Kjartan and his nephew and foster son Bolli, the saga surges forward into other stories of love and conflict, journeys and generations, down all the days. The beautiful Gudrun, Kjartan's lover, eventually marries his foster brother Bolli and then, in a fit of jealously, goads Bolli into killing Kjartan. This sets in motion a serial of vengeance, quite unaffected by the Christianity Iceland embraced in the year 1000 when Kjartan returned from Norway, a convert to the new faith. Gudrun's tragic history includes the shipwreck and drowning of two of her four husbands. The rhythm of the saga is like the rhythm of the long waves of the ocean, rising and falling, rising and falling.

The *Laxdæla Saga* was composed by an unknown author in the middle of the thirteenth century. It made its appearance at the time when the crusades had made Jerusalem once more a place of pilgrimage, when Franciscans and Dominicans were purifying Christendom from heresy, when the troubadours of the age of chivalry sang ballads at the courts of southern Europe. Towards the end of the saga Bolli Bollason, the son Gudrun bore after the revenge killing of her husband Bolli, journeys to Constantinople, where for several years he enlists in the service of the Varangian Guard, the élite Scandinavian bodyguard of the Byzantine emperors. And in the closing lines of the saga it is recorded that as an old man Gellir Thorkelsson,

was so much conjecture. Some say Thule was Iceland, others the Faeroes or even Scandinavia. Its name goes back to a Greek called Pytheas of Marseille, and the voyage he made there in 330 BC. According to his reports Ultima Thule was Unst, the north island of Shetland, which he considered to be the most northerly inhabited country in Europe.

The *Motor Vessel St Clair*, on which I sailed from Aberdeen to Lerwick, left harbour ten hours late for its twelve hour journey. It is the third *M V St Clair* to link Lerwick with mainland Scotland since the steamer service was set up 130 years ago, and not the most beautiful. Next morning the fierce November gales which had delayed the sailing were still unrolling wave after long uncompromising wave from the Atlantic. The surge of the ocean swell, rising and falling like some macrocosmic respiration, formed endlessly reforming heights and troughs where the white gulls skimming the surface of the dark sea played hide and seek with my eyes.

Orkney and Shetland were part of the Danish Princess Margaret's dowry when she married the future James III of Scotland in 1469. Links between the islands and the rest of Europe soon developed. Since Viking times Lerwick's harbour had offered shelter to sailors from Iceland and Scandinavia, Scotland and continental Europe. In the seventeenth century Dutch fishermen discovered that the Bressay Sound between Lerwick and the isle of Bressay was an ideal haven for their squat lugsail ships. They assembled before the Feast of John the Baptist on June 24 when the herring season started. Trade sprang up with the local people, fresh meat and knitted woolen goods for tea, spirits and tobacco. St James's Day, July 25, marked the end of the season, by when the silver mine to the east of Shetland had yielded its riches for another year. 'Amsterdam was built oot o' the back o' Bressay,' they used to say. It wasn't until the late nineteenth century that Shetlanders themselves began fishing the shoals of herring off their coasts. More than a million barrels of salted herring were eventually shipped each year to markets in Germany, Russia and elsewhere, until the First World War put an end to all that.

One of my hosts, the minister of Sandwick and Dunrossness, was a Shetlander by birth. An amateur photographer, he had a valuable collection of framed photographs and postcards of Shetland by a well-known pre-war photographer, J D Rattar. Rattar's portraits and photographs of land and seascapes, crofts and townships, are a fascinating record of the history and geography of the islands. One

1930s photograph, subtitled 'Street Musicians, Lerwick' in J D Rattar's elegant hand, shows a group of three musicians playing in Commercial Street outside his shop—a violinist, guitarist, drum and cymbals player—and a boy singing. The guitarist was my host's father.

Another photo was of a boatbuilder's yard in Lerwick under a sky banked with cumulus. Bressay is across the water in the background. A single herring drifter with its distinctive smokestack is steaming up the sound. The yard is cluttered with trestles, planks and beams of wood. In the dock two trawlers with their tackle laid out on deck await repairs. A couple of Shetland yawls—open, clinker-built, with pointed bows and sterns—lie on their sides in the foreground. Two men inspect the work which has to be done.

There was ice on the little Loch of Brindister on the Sunday morning in mid-November when I drove up the road from Sandwick to Gulberwick. My borrowed car, having been parked in the open, had been difficult to start. But the day was fine, the sea sparkled with natural good humour, and the Shetland winter landscape south of Lerwick looked much less driech than I had seen it, in spite of the messy anarchy of its scattered houses.

Gulberwick church was built at the beginning of the century as an extension charge of the parish church in Lerwick. It is a simple stone and slate-roofed building standing in a walled churchyard by the shore. No spire or belfry. From the roadside you have to walk the length of the church to reach the entrance which is at the other end. Its only door faces south-east, to the sea.

Two tiny rooms beside the door serve as vestry and Sunday school classroom. And coffee is served there after the service. The sturdy pews were made for a congregation of over a hundred, almost ten times too many for today. But the folk there that morning, women, children, old men, were so welcoming I wished I could have stayed a while instead of hurrying off for the next service in Lerwick.

*   *   *

Before the Whalsay ferry rounds the headland of The Taing at the mouth of Vidlin Voe, over to the west on Lunna Ness, you can pick out a sturdy, eighteenth century church by the shore. It is Lunna Kirk. Stunted sycamore trees grow between its stout buttresses, like the lining of a winter coat, shaped to the masonry by the wind. Nearby

Lunna House, the headquarters of the 'Shetland Bus' and the Norwegian Resistance during World War II, stands naked and lonely on the stark landscape.

Whalsay is the most prosperous fishing island of the archipelago, but it still has ninety-two crofts for a population of about a thousand, each with rights to the common pasture on the hill. A big debate was going on about the profitability of rearing sheep in Shetland. A flock of lambs had been sold at market for 10 pence each! Would the European Commission subsidize farmers who culled their lambs to save on winter fodder? The debate is one more illustration of Panikkar's Law, how promising policies set in motion at the micro level later develop an impact and scale that is unnatural and disastrous.

The session clerk of the kirk, who was a retired headmaster of the island school, took me round the island. We visited his grandfather's croft where he cures mutton in the same way as his grandfather did for wedding parties and funerals. Besides his sheep he is introducing pigs. The Shetland ponies he rears sell well to breeders in the Netherlands. He plants kale in his planticrubs, the stone walled enclosures like miniature sheepfolds where the cabbage is seeded in autumn. His potato rigs, stretching down to the sea on the relatively sheltered side of the island are amongst the few strip fields in Shetland still used for cultivation.

We visited the thick-walled Whalsay church, the only church on the island—one building, one denomination. It stands on the isolated headland of Kirk Ness surrounded by a graveyard and the sea, more a reminder of what the Christian faith meant for a struggling community in the past, than a relevant symbol for the islanders of today. A high gallery crowds out the church interior, jutting over rows of tall, box pews, as if the function of observer of the cult were to dominate the celebration. The congregation finds the church too cold in winter, so from November to March they meet in a modern hall in Symbister.

The seven super trawlers in Symbister harbour, their berths near the sixteenth century Pier House built for German merchants of the Hanseatic League, leave an indelible impression of the change over two generations in Whalsay's way with nature. I was shown around the *Antares* by its skipper, 'one of the richest men on Whalsay,' according to my host. It was built a year or two ago in Flekkefjord in Norway for a cost of over £7 million, equipped with the latest in navigational, meteorological and communications technology. The computer retrieval system on the chart screen recaptured the course of its most recent fishing trip in an instant. In the vast 'wheel house' there is no wheel to steer by any more, just a lever the size of your thumb for the captain in his executive armchair to manipulate in case the automatic pilot isn't operating. Satellites have long superseded the stars. The constellations are as outmoded now for navigation as their mythical names became for religion in high antiquity (though how wonderfully starlit the cold clear nights in Shetland were).

The ten-man crew of the super trawler all enjoy five-star accommodation. They are fishermen, though it seems that they hardly touch a fish. Computer operators rather, they watch them being engineered on board. The *Antares* discharges its catch of mackerel in Norway, Lerwick or Aberdeen, wherever the price is best. It respects the EC quotas perhaps, but, with its sophisticated nets and suction pipes, in fact it is constructed to empty the sea of pelagic fish. The skipper, a gentle, quiet-spoken Whalsayman, would like eventually to fish in the South Atlantic off West Africa. International regulations won't hamper him there in his task, which is effectively the technologically managed extermination of fish in the sea.

*   *   *

The oil terminal of Sullom Voe is the biggest installation of its kind in Europe, a pillar of European economic, technological civilisation: over six billion barrels of crude oil produced in twenty years. The safeguards against environmental pollution agreed with the Shetland Islands Council before it started operations in 1981 go far beyond what is laid down by international protocols. Talk about 'oil spill prevention', 'pollution response' and 'environmental monitoring' is an important aspect of the industry's effort to integrate technocracy into the mind set of society. While I was visiting the terminal, they brought in a rig supply ship, built for the North Atlantic, with its massive steel bows staved in by a freak wave during the storm a few days before. But in spite of such constant reminders of the power of wind and waves there is little talk of them as alternative sources of energy. It would have been regarded as naive or impertinent of me to suggest it. Sullom Voe's public relations policy avoids fundamentals. It focuses on dealing with the consequences and limiting the negative effects of technocratic culture. 'Gannets typify the local sea bird communities which the terminal's environmental procedures are designed to protect', says the propaganda alongside a photo of a gannet colony—rather than 'Gannets typify the local sea bird communities which the oil industry radically threatens.' Power over hearts and minds belongs to those who manipulate the signs and symbols.

My kind guide, an environmental security officer, knew Sullom Voe like the back of his hand. He had spent all his life working for BP, including some years on the rigs. After lunch he was driving me round the plant in a Land Rover, explaining chemical processes, storage procedures, security measures and the efforts taken to protect the habitat of ottars. In the evening he and I were huddled around an oil heater with a Bible-study group in the church where he was an elder, reading John's Gospel together.

The way the secular and the religious overlap in Shetland is remarkable. It makes for an integrated way of life which is increasingly rare today. People are open and generous in ordinary affairs. But perhaps it has also allowed changes in specific areas of culture to creep up on Christian faith and catch it unawares. Christian ethics has become imprisoned within the larger closed circle of secular ideology (technocratic, capitalist, etc), and the church has hardly noticed. Its good conscience has not been affected.

How can one raise basic questions such as: Are there limits to this technology? Where is 'development' leading? Has a focus on efficiency completely done away with the concept of sufficiency, the idea that enough's enough? It would require time and mutual trust to raise such questions. But that surely is one of the things the local church is there for. The fact is that it is more sacrilegious to challenge society's beliefs about technology and 'development' than to question the creed and theology of the Christian faith.

If 'development', as Gilbert Rist puts it, is the belief that 'the "good life" can be assured for all through technological progress and ever-rising production of goods and services—from which everyone will eventually benefit',[5] who can deny that the Shetland Islands are highly 'developed'? Shetland offers an extraordinarily clear illustration of the post-war western ideology of 'development' in action. Its isolated island status, limited size and small population (20,000) focus the case.

---

[5] Gilbert Rist, *The History of Development: from Western Origins to Global Faith*, trans. Patrick Camiller, Zed Books, 1997, p. 14.

A combination of foresight and careful management on the part of the Shetland Islands Council—natural resources, available capital, the latest technology—and the meteoric growth in people's general material well-being, all confirm the example.

Moreover, it is poverty that is regarded as a scandal, never wealth. Christians and other people of good will find it morally unacceptable that 'development' should be limited to us, to Shetlanders, to the West. And so another article of western faith, the obligation to care for the alien and the poor, is transformed into the duty to promote 'development'. Though the failure of successive UN development decades has proven time and time again the impossibility of exporting 'development' to other continents and cultures without deeply noxious effects, it is still affirmed as the panacea for the world.

But there are undeniable signs that the era of 'development' is drawing to an end. In the case of the *Antares*, the construction of super trawlers on the one hand and dwindling fish stocks on the other are an obvious example of the failure of an economic management approach to nature. If the prosperous, environmentally friendly image of Sullom Voe is more difficult for Shetlanders to see through, it is only so because the impact of the technocratic civilisation it represents is not as obvious here as, for example, in the case of Shell in Nigeria, or the debacle of the Gulf War. There is a *parfum de fin du monde* about the smell of both fish and oil in Shetland.

Has the church no counter-culture to challenge the deep convictions of *homo occidentalis*? Can the Bible not illumine what the cult of 'development' prevents us from seeing?

> Never since the world began has it been heard that anyone opened the eyes of a man born blind ...
> ... he spat on the ground and made clay of the spittle and anointed the man's eyes with the clay, saying to him, 'Go, wash in the pool of Siloam' (which means Sent) ...
> '... one thing I know, that though I was blind, now I see ...'[6]

The essential demands concern things which are invisible

---

[6] John 9: 32, 6-7, 25.

from the economist's viewpoint ... the radical loss brought
on by the process of 'development' and which no surfeit
of merchandise or money can compensate.

... there are only two serious questions. The first is *to
know how it is possible to see what our customary way of
understanding the world hinders us from seeing.* The second ...
how to take seriously what, for economic thought, cannot exist
(and, inversely, but it comes to the same thing, how to
stop believing in the reality of things that don't exist) ...[7]

For judgement I came into this world, that those who do
not see may see, and that those who see may become
blind ...[8]

*   *   *

The first snow of winter had laid the top of Ronas Hill with a light
covering of white which set store upon the faded greens and browns
and ochres of the north Mainland moors and challenged the rich
greys of cloud and sea and voe. A couple of swans in a flash of
sunlight on the surface of a nearby loch had the same sumptuous
effect. I was on the road from Brae through Northmaven to Esha
Ness.

The Esha Ness lighthouse stands at the southern end of a
mile of crumbling flat-topped cliffs and clefts and stacks, pounded by
the ocean's swell, alive with birds. In the distance, through the spume
that shrouds the broken promontory, rises the *Grind o' da Navir*, the
Gateway of the Giants, bearing witness to Shetland's awesome original
myth of the nature of the North Atlantic.

---

[7]   Gilbert Rist, Majid Rahnema and Gustavo Esteva: *Le Nord perdu—Repères pour l'après-développement*, Editions d'en bas, Lausanne, 1992, p.86, my translation.

[8]   John 9: 39.

Are you not the wild goose?

The sea was calm and the weather fair as the *Clansman* quit the Sound of Mull and passed the Point of Ardnamurchan. To the north were the dusky shapes of Muck and Eigg, Rum, Canna and Skye; to the south, the Treshnish Isles, Staffa, Coll and eventually, Tiree. Ahead was the Sea of the Hebrides. Then the wind rose, blowing from the direction of a wind rose somewhere north of Skye. It whipped the swell into little waves. On the choppy water out ahead a flock of shearwaters took off to right and left as the ship approached, flying fast and low through troughs and over waves, shearing the water, changing course and switching colour from sleek black back to vivid white breast like tumblers in a circus. The shearwater is the tomboy cousin of the fulmar.

By the time the ferry had called at Castlebay and was toiling north to Lochboisdale, Boreas was blowing at force six. The saltire flying from the prow was at full stretch. A watery sun, as if embarrassed by the failing fortunes of the summer weather, lay low over Barra and Eriskay. Great rollers flexed their way south, like the taught muscles of the earth. The huge box of a boat seemed timed to ride half a dozen waves, mount one and beat down with its flat bottom on the next in a torrent of spray, with all the thud and shudder of landing on solid ground. At church next day a man told me a story of a ship crashing through such seas, which ended with the remark, 'It's a very low tide today!'

Howmore Church was built in 1854 beside the ruins of a twelvth or thirteenth century chapel. South Uist is that kind of historical mix. The architecture of the present church is simple, with a central pulpit and rear gallery. What's special about the interior is its long communion table flanked by box pews, running lengthwise down the middle of the church. There are only two or three like it left in Scotland. It was Communion Sunday, one of three in the year, and the table was covered with a white cloth. At the appropriate moment in the service the communicants took their places at the table. There was a common cup for the wine.

The service was in English but in the vestry afterwards the

elders spoke amongst themselves in Gaelic. The minister with whom I was staying was a lowlander like me. His wife told me how difficult it was for her to participate in social activities in Daliburgh because of her lack of Gaelic. And yet the Gaelic is increasingly threatened now. Mary, the former postmistress of Howmore and Howbeg whom we fetched to church by car, said she needed the English, 'otherwise I can't speak to my grandchildren when they come up from London.' And she hasn't been replaced since she retired.

Until after the First World War, I learned, a fishing trip to the Monach Isles, eight miles out in the Atlantic, would last from Monday to Saturday. A boat, just over twenty feet in length with four of a crew, would carry an iron pot with a peat fire in it, placed on the flagstone ballast. Besides the creels and fishing tackle, there would be peat for the fire and a week's provisions of potatoes, eggs, oatcakes, butter, cheese, tea, sugar and drinking water. Potatoes and freshly caught fish were boiled in salt water. There was always a Bible on board to be read night and morning.

According to a local gloss on the Gospel story, Jesus once commanded the fishermen disciples, Peter, Andrew, James and John, to row out into the Sea of Galilee to cast their nets where they would find fish for hungry people. So the hardy Uist fishermen would take their boats and row out into the Atlantic at Christmas time to cast their nets. The fish they caught were called the Christmas Tribute and were given as alms to the poorest people on the island.

*   *   *

Some of the housing at the Balivanich base looks like a run-down, post-war council estate, with many of the houses empty and boarded up. It must be a bleak place in winter. The army and air force presence has been cut back, its work subcontracted by the Ministry of Defence to the Defence Evaluation and Research Agency (DERA). Only a few military personnel remain.

'We still fire missiles at America,' said Crawford with a smile; my host at the Officers' Mess was the second in command, a lieutenant colonel, 'that's our job.' He waved towards the oil painting that had caught my eye in the lobby of the Mess, a dramatic scene from the heyday of the Ranges in which a company of soldiers are busy at a jetty loading a launch with boxes of ammunition and artillery shells, while another craft has put to sea under smoking missiles which streak away into the distance.

The talk in the bar was about golf and fishing and the golden eagles on Benbecula. An affable young radar officer turned out to be the nephew of an old friend of mine. He had served in the Falklands, and from what I gathered, spent much of his time there fishing the well-stocked rivers for rosy trout. 'They might well have been golden eagles,' he told me when I described what I had seen on my afternoon walk along the beach. 'The way you tell is by their wingtips. The feathers are like turned-up fingers.'

What I missed in the conversation was any discussion about the war in Kosovo which was ending amid complex negotiations between NATO and its former Cold War enemy, Russia. Maybe my hosts had debated it *ad nauseam*. I was still coming to terms with the conflict in my own mind between sympathy for NATO's action as a last defence of human rights, and horror at the destruction and technological alienation of the bombing campaign. There was not the political hypocricy behind the war in Kosovo that there was with the Gulf War. But the absence of discussion about it made me uneasy, as if I were there under false pretences.

I had breakfast in the Mess with some DERA personnel, up from the south of England. A woman who had come to check on the productivity of her staff was understandably more excited about the prospects of a trip to St Kilda. 'Last stop before America,' one of the old hands was telling her. 'You're lucky. You'll be out there in less than half an hour on a day like this.'

Later that morning, Crawford invited me home to his house at Tigharry in North Uist. As we left the Officers' Mess the daily helicopter flight to St Kilda which was under his command roared overhead. We had coffee with Linda, his wife, who had accompanied me to a meeting in the church hall the night before. I admired the way they had converted their old croft. The sitting room window looked out at St Kilda which seemed surprisingly close.

'You can watch all the weather fronts as they come in from the Atlantic,' Crawford told me. 'I'm happy to pass on that one,' I replied. It was a glorious day, quite enough meteorological novelty for me. Just south of them across the bay was a nature reserve with all kinds of birds. 'Permanent residents of course,' Linda was the bird watcher, 'but many are just passing through.' Crawford and Linda themselves came from Glasgow, but like most professional soldiers and their families, had travelled the world. When they first came to Balivanich they were just passing through, posted to the periphery for a few years. The second time, they decided to stay. 'This is home now,' Linda said, 'we love it on Uist. When Crawford retires we won't be leaving.'

Crawford drove me to the ferry at Otternish in his open sports car, an extravaganza I greatly enjoyed. Here were two grey-haired fifty-somethings, one quite distinctive in camouflage kit, bowling along in the sun and the wind on a single-track road in the Outer Hebrides at all of thirty-five miles an hour. Past the Scolpaig Tower (another folly), and carpets of wild pinks by the Vallay Strand, to where rough grass is growing again on a hill which was gutted to supply the rock for the new causeway to Berneray. On the way a barn owl surprised us by the roadside, its measured flight, soft plumage and heart-shaped face unmistakable in the daylight. Hold on, I thought, barn owls are mainland birds. What's a barn owl doing on a moorland in North Uist? But then I could hardly believe I was there myself!

*   *   *

The ferry from Otternish to Leverburgh weaves its way across the Sound of Harris between islands and shoals, rocks and skerries. In the pocket of my anorak I had a booklet entitled *Sea-Names of Berneray* by a certain Donald MacKillop of Berneray, an offprint of the *Transactions of the Gaelic Society of Inverness*. It records the meaning of the names of rocks and islands in the Sound of Harris, and the memories they represent which have been 'folded away'. It was written a few years ago from the author's own experience, his knowledge of the Gaelic, and conversations with the older generation of islanders. Already, he laments, 'a lot of names are lost forever.'[1]

Donald MacKillop's first entry is about Sgeir an Leusain (Skerry of the Little Light), a rock off the coast of North Uist. He tells the story of a sea-fowling trip made by three men from Berneray about one hundred years ago, when two of them became stranded on the skerry as a storm blew up. The third man raised the alarm on Berneray

---

[1] Donald MacKillop, *Sea-Names of Berneray*, reprinted from *Transactions of the Gaelic Society of Inverness*, Vol. LVI, 1990, p. 2.

and 'a sturdy boat was selected along with a crew of strong young men, who set out, in total darkness into the eye of the storm, to rescue the stranded fowlers on Sgeir an Leusain. No mean feat of navigation in the darkness ... They had matches and guns in their possession and when they estimated that they were in the vicinity of this rock, they fired a volley of shots. They got an immediate reply from the stranded men, who fired their guns and answered their shouts. Matches were lit and the boat guided on to the rock. The stranded men were rescued with only seconds to spare. They were up to their elbows in the sea and holding on to each other ...' MacKillop makes the point that the third man 'knew the name of the skerry concerned and the rescue crew knew its approximate position, even in the darkness ... Undoubtedly the local system of naming every shoal, rock and island paved the way for a very speedy rescue. This system is still used in the islands and no national grid reference can improve on it ...'[2]

The same almost instinctive connection between culture and nature comes out in another entry explaining the translation of the name of a bay on Harris, Camus an Liubhaire, as Bay of the Rescue. He puts it in the context of a verse set to a bagpipe tune from 'a very old song from Uist', which was given him by an octogenarian called Malcolm, son of Norman, son of Malcolm MacLeod. 'There is nothing in it but place names,' he writes, 'yet the sound of the names in Gaelic and the manner in which they are sung shows a profound relationship between its music and the elements and man and his environment. This relationship is utterly lost when the words are transmuted to another language.'

All the same he gives an English translation of the verse which to my mind does preserve something of the geopoetics of the original.

> *Fraoch a Ronaigh*
> Heisgeir, Haisgeir, Dubh sgeir Rònaigh
> Culaibh Phabaigh, 's Gob an Tòa,
> Camus an Liuhaire, agus Sodhaigh
> Far an tric a' chròic an éirigh.
> Beinn Dubh Shollais, Aird a' Mhorain,
> Cnoc nan Torran, 's fad 'o chéil' iad,

---

[2] *Op. cit.*, pp. 15, 16.

Càirinnis, Grìminnis, Iollairigh, Bearnaraigh,
Fraoch a Rònaigh, muran a Bhàlaigh.

Heather from Ronay
Heisgeir, Haisgeir, Black skerry of Ronay,
Back of Pabay and point of Toe,
Bay of delivery, Isle of Soay,
Where the foaming breakers rise.
Black Ben of Sollas, Aird of Moran,
Knoll of Hillocks, all far apart.
Carinish, Griminish, Iollary, Berneray,
Heather from Ronay, sea-bent from Valay.[3]

In his search for the wild swans of northern Japan, Kenneth White writes about 'how, in the eighteenth century, the last time deep questions were put in a *public* way, the swans were at the centre of the debate concerning wildness and domesticity, the civilised and the primitive, the rude and the cultivated ... back there in the eighteenth century, you had that general discipline called "natural philosophy", before all the specialisms, a discipline in which poetry, science and philosophy come together, and where an *overall* questioning is to the fore, and the search for a global comprehension, a global conscious experience.'[4]

The Fairway of the Swan (Seolaid na h-Eala) runs from the Minch, between islands and skerries close to Uist, past the jetty at Otternish. Its course is charted by Donald MacKillop. The channel used to continue through the Sound of Berneray and out by Boreray to the Atlantic, until a few months ago when the causeway to Berneray cut it off. I scanned the shoreline for swans as the ferry set off. But the swan in question (so I read) was the name of a *birlinn*, or galley, which was built over three hundred years ago in Skye. She was a pirate ship which raided and plundered in the islands and was eventually lost on a trip to Uist!

So, no swans this time, but in the middle of the ferry crossing a crow, high up, making steadfastly for the other side, as the crow flies.

---

[3] *Op. cit.*, pp. 27, 28.
[4] Kenneth White, *Pilgrim of the Void, Travels in South-East Asia and the North Pacific*, Mainstream, Edinburgh, 1992, pp. 243, 245.

And there were gannets, single and in companies of up to five or six, patrolling the waterway:

> Noonday excursion from St Kilda,
> a timeless expedition to survive—
> the unhurried rhythm
> of the gannet's flight
> disturbs
> the culture-cluttered nature
> of our lives.

As the ferry approached Leverburgh, a flock of wild geese flew alongside, jostling for position in a ragged V. They overtook the vessel and, circling twice, settled on the foreshore not far from the jetty. 'Are you not the wild goose?' they used to say in Berneray of someone who was particularly fine and strong. 'Are you not the wild goose?' I whispered to the wild geese in reply.

*   *   *

I had bed and breakfast at a Mrs Slater's in Stornoway. The news in Gaelic was on the kitchen radio when I came down in the morning. She had prepared a substantial breakfast for me. When I was ready to go I paid the bill and she gave me change in crisp new £1 notes. 'I made them myself this morning,' she said.

Walking along the water front in the gardens of Lews Castle I noted down the trees. Almost a dozen species: oak, ash, beech, elm, sycamore, pine, fir, birch, alder, rowan and elder. The trees there are unique in the Outer Isles. It was June and the rhododendron was in bloom.

From the castle grounds I noticed an old sailing boat, standing high on her keel in the mud at low tide, tied up against the dock of the inner harbour. The lines of her hull were beautiful though an ugly aluminium wheelhouse had been added to the deck. The woodwork from bow to stern had been stripped of paint, ready for a new coat. As I went along Cromwell Street and passed the ship's berth, a man in overalls came up from below. He turned out to be the owner. I enquired where the boat came from. 'From Norway,' he told me, 'I sailed her over in the hope of refitting her, but the job's too much for me. I'm going to have to sell her.' He wondered if I were interested.

Stornoway Town Hall was preparing for an art and poetry exhibition, called 'Green Waters', of the work of Ian Stephen and Ian Hamilton Finlay, whose poem, composed from the names of fishing boats, gave the exhibition its name. I was kindly invited in for a preview.

Green Waters
Blue Spray
Grayfish

Anna T
Karen B
Netta Croan

Constant Star
Daystar
Starwood

Starlit Waters
Moonlit Waters
Drift

*   *   *

The Minch was calm. A Nimrod flew across the ferry's bows. A frigate was steaming south between the Shiant Isles and Skye. Military manoeuvres were under way. This was the day the K-FOR troops were to start their entry into Kosovo. The company of two schools of dolphins on the crossing added an imponderable lightness to the day.

The coastline of Sutherland took shape slowly in the distance. At first the rugged blue-grey panorama is no more than a dark stripe on the horizon, separating the vast sea from the enormous sky. From Cape Wrath to Point of Stoer the headlands are faint and blurred. But as the ferry ploughs across the fifty miles of Minch from Stornoway to Ullapool *'this frieze of mountains, filed/ on the blue air'*, as Norman MacCaig calls it, becomes more and more distinct. The landscape rears up out of the sea to take on an aspect of magnificent intransigence. From Assynt to Achiltibuie, Quinag, Ben More, Canisp, Suilven, Cul Mor, Cul Beag, Stac Polly—the mountains tower over the broken coast. The Summer Isles which guard the entrance to Loch Broom are meagre left-overs of rock and heather washed by the sea.

Part Three

Of the welter a world that will last

Is it true, prince, that you said once that 'beauty' will save the world?
Gentlemen! ... the prince asserts that beauty will save the world! But I
assert that the reason he has such playful ideas is that he is in love ...
What sort of beauty will save the world?

Dostoevsky, *The Idiot*

*   *   *

. . . .
               for the question is always
                  how
               out of all the chances and changes
             to select
          the features of real significance
                              so as to make
                of the welter
                   a world that will last
          and how to order
                        the signs and the symbols
               so they will continue
                  to form new patterns
               developing into
          new harmonic wholes
                        so to keep life alive
             in complexity
                and complicity
                              with all of being—
       there is only poetry

Kenneth White, *Walking the coast.*

Nocturne after the age of Chopin

During the eighteenth and nineteenth centuries most direct protests against social injustice were in prose. They were reasoned arguments written in the belief that, given time, people would come to see reason, and that, finally, history was on the side of reason. Today this is by no means clear. The outcome is by no means guaranteed. The suffering of the present and the past is unlikely to be redeemed by a future era of universal happiness. And evil is a constant ineradicable reality. All this means that the resolution—the coming to terms with the sense to be given to life—cannot be deferred. The future cannot be trusted. The moment of truth is now. And more and more it will be poetry, rather than prose, that receives this truth. Prose is far more trusting than poetry; poetry speaks to the immediate wound.[1]

Whenever I'm in Lisbon I take one of those rickety little trams that rattle along the waterfront out to Belém on the west side of the city. Belém is on the coast where the great River Tagus opens to the sea. It was from Belém that the Portuguese sailors and explorers set out in their carracks and caravels five hundred years ago on their voyages of discovery. Vasco da Gama is buried in the exquisite Monastery Church of the Geronimos which flanks the square facing the shore. On the other side is the estuary and then the ocean, reaching away towards the south and west as far as the eye can see.

When Manuel I became King of Portugal in 1495, he asked the Pope to authorize the building of a monastery. It was to be on the site of the Chapel of Our Lady of Bethlehem, built thirty-five years earlier by Henry the Navigator as a sanctuary for sailors about to set out into the unknown. The stone used for the monastery is a warm limestone from Setubal, south of the Tagus. The architecture is

---

[1] John Berger, *And Our Faces, My Heart, Brief as Photos*, Vintage Books, New York, 1991, p. 95.

'Manueline'—strength and grace combined. Its domed tower is topped by King Manuel's insignia, the cross and the globe, which dominate the square.

Or rather, they used to dominate it—until 1992. The monastery now shares its commanding position with another massive building on the west side of the square, the new Cultural Centre of Belém. It was built for the European Council during Portugal's Presidency of the Community in the early nineties. Although not as expensive as the 5 percent of the initial takings of the Discoveries, which was the cost of the monastery, it represents a huge investment for the government, which is heavily subsidised, anxious to please, and in hot pursuit of the liberal economic ideal of the European Community. Seen from the sea, the Cultural Centre looks more like a prison than a council chamber and concert hall. The few windows on its side walls are high up and small. The roof is flat. The effect is like a fortress.

In the second half of the fifteenth century, the culture of mediaeval Europe was no longer adequate to face the new questions of existence. Radical change was necessary. It was this that led artists to imagine a new theory of perspective, sailors and architects to design caravels which could sail the Atlantic, astronomers and geographers to prove the earth was round and had no Mediterranean fulcrum any more in Rome or in Jerusalem.

The late twentieth century has also been a time of enormous discovery and change. Science suggests that there is an answer for all the problems of existence—as long as there's someone to pay the bill. Economics is the organising principle of the day, which is why the European Union has such an important role to stabilise an uncertain world.

But the power and domination reflected in both buildings in Belém are the same. Facing the ocean, the monastery defended and propagated the faith, the Cultural Centre protects and promotes economic wealth. The terms 'savages' for the former, and 'developing countries' for the latter, define each in their own way how 'the other' across the sea is perceived.

But there's a difference between the Monastery of the Geronimos and the Cultural Centre of Belém. Increasing uncertainty, even menace, is in the air today. Our economic model threatens two things, nature and justice. Institutions call them 'environment' and 'development' since these concepts are more manageable. But the contradiction between the rhythm of nature on the one hand, and the culture of economic growth (without which, it is argued, there will be no justice for the 'developing' countries) on the other, is rooted in the system, and unavoidable. It's very simple really. Without growth economic, industrial civilisation will grind to a halt; with more growth nature and everything we love in it will slowly pass away.

*   *   *

When I lived in Geneva, my office was up behind the headquarters of the UN and the WCC, in an elegant country house, standing in a park. One Saturday when I was there alone, I noticed some people arriving in the gardens, laden with equipment—wires, ropes, lights, posts and stakes, sledge hammers, wrenches and other tools. They hung around awhile discussing things, obviously choosing a place on the lawn—between flowerbeds, away from trees, visible from all sides. Then they began to rig up a tightrope, thirty feet above the ground, anchored and guyed, with a mounting gradient at each end. That evening after dark there was to be a performance of Jean Genet's 'The Tightrope Walker'.

Genet's *Le Funambule* is not a play. It's a meditation offered to the artiste about his art. It was performed that night (I stayed to watch) by a tightrope walker, interrupting and accompanying his high wire act with the words of the essay spoken as one long soliloquay.

> I wouldn't be surprised when you walk on the ground if you fell and twisted your ankle. *(He begins speaking on the ground.)* The wire will carry you better, more safely than a road ...
>
> The love—almost despairing but full of tenderness—that you must show for your wire *(he takes his balancing rod and begins to mount the long slow slope)*, this love will have as much strength as the wire has to carry you ... Your leaps and bounds, your dances ... you will complete not so that you shine, but so that a steel wire which was dead and voiceless finally sings ... Death—the Death I am telling you about—is not the one which follows your fall, but the one which precedes your

appearance on the wire … One is not an artiste except that some *great grief is mixed with it* …

If I advise you to avoid luxury in your private life … it is so that this distance from an obvious poverty to the most splendid apparition leads to such a tension that the dance will be like a release or a cry, it's because the reality of the Circus is contained in this metamorphosis of dust into gold dust … *(In the darkness the arc lights illumine his glittering figure as he begins to leap and dance on the wire.)*

You enter, and you are alone. Apparently, for God is there. I have no idea where he comes from and perhaps you brought him as you entered, or the solitude aroused him, it's all the same. It's for him that you are chasing your image …

What God am I talking about? I wonder myself. But he is complete absence of critique and judgement …[2]

*   *   *

Behind the monastery, on the hillside above Vilemov, where the forest ends and the stubble fields begin their long descent to the plain, you can see as far as Olomouc and the foothills of the Carpathian Mountains where Moravia gives way to Slovakia. Away to the left, the September rainclouds beat their way down from the north, like successive hoards of peoples on the move, obscuring farms and forests, forcing a passage across the rich countryside. A shaft of sunlight on the city illuminates its yellow ochre palaces, its seminaries, domes and towers, and—at a remove, amongst dark trees—Zlaty Kopecek, the Golden Hill with its church and cloister, the Moravian Escurial.

The original fortress of Olomouc was built here in the thirteenth century, on a plain where trade routes crossed between west and east and north and south, linking Burgundy and the Black Sea, the Baltic and the Balkans. Control of the crossroads brought with it revenues enough for Olomouc to build its baroque monuments, its churches, squares and famous fountains.

---

[2] Jean Genet, *Œuvres complètes*, Gallimard, Paris, 1979, pp. 9-27, my translation.

This is the hub of Europe, the mid point of the continent. The lovely girl who sang for us at the party last night was Czech, working with migrants in Olomouc. The accordianist and his tambourine-playing son were Armenian refugees. Between them they sang songs from Armenia, Romania, Bulgaria, Bohemia, Moravia, Slovakia, Ukraine—songs about nature and history, love and war; many tunes and many languages, but the same emotions. The soldier who curses the French for killing his brother at Austerlitz, the priest accused not for his womanizing but for his hypocrisy, the jilted lover. And the liturgical songs of the three shy nuns from Romania, who were prevailed upon to sing as the evening advanced, sounded much the same. My warm glow wasn't just from the home-made slivovitz!

The road up the hill behind the monastery passed through orchards of ripe apples, pears and walnuts. The cherries, plums and mirabels had been harvested already. The trees in the forest were oak, beech, fir, pine, and at the edges elder and rowan, laden with berries. The blackberries in the undergrowth were the sweetest I could remember. As I walked along the line where the woods end and the fields begin, I came across a fawn, soft, dappled, beautiful, curled up on the stubble field as if it were asleep. But it was dead.

Less to conquer than to be a sign

Warning: if a congregation has no conception of spiritual humour,
if it has no sense of irony and has quite generally failed to discover
the secret of laughter, it is perhaps better to let this material lie ...
'Can a minister too be saved?'—this should be an agonizing
question for ministers and for all members of the church who
know very well what the truth is.[1]

A wintry Sunday evening in the heart of old Brussels; cold, bitterly cold, and no warmer inside the great church than out. Just enough light to be struck by the emptiness of the interior—huge grey stone pillars rising laboriously to the high ceiling, great uneven flagstones for the floor, no pews or seats, no rude screen or gilded ornaments around the altar—unusually bare for a baroque Catholic church. One elaborate piece of furniture spoils the space. Beneath the pulpit there is a life-sized wooden sculpture of Saint Dominic, cross in hand, placing a triumphant foot on the back of a Moor who has fallen to the ground. A serpent issues from the Koran in the dust under the Moor's head. As a Christian symbol in modern times it is an embarrassment. And St Dominic never had such relations with Muslims anyway! A simple crucifix hangs on a nearby wall.

But it's as if there are squatters in the empty church. In the middle of the broad nave, a long table has been set lengthways with a clean white cloth, flowers, candles and Bible. A score of assorted heaters with large gas bottles, their high double mantels like the fiery wings of angels struggling to stay aloft in the gloom, are trained on the place where a little crowd of people has already begun to sit down in a ring of chairs. A spotlight picks out a reading desk. A microphone is being tested so that a voice might be heard in the ecclesiastical void.

St Jean-Baptiste au Béguinage was built by the Jesuits during the Counter-Reformation on the ruins of an earlier church destroyed

---

[1] Kornelis H Miskotte, *When the Gods are Silent*, Collins, London, 1967, pp. 422, 425.

by the Reformers. As the style and scale of the architecture suggest, its construction was by then more of a symbol of regained Roman Catholic supremacy than a place for the dwindling beguine community to worship. The beguines were laywomen in the Middle Ages, young and old, including widows and single mothers with children, who lived in communities that were less regulated than the religious orders and largely outwith the control of the hierarchy. In Louvain, Lier or Bruges the Beguine Convents, with their rows of little independent houses surrounded by protective walls, are to this day well-preserved reminders of a form of Christian community peculiar to northern Europe. Only a few houses from the Brussels *Béguinage* survive, but today's grassroots community of St John the Baptist reflects the beguines' independent life-style in another age.

We were there to celebrate the installation of the new *curé* of the parish. Jean-Mathieu is an unusual Jesuit. For some time he has been a member of the pastoral team which runs the parish. For the last twenty-five years he has also been a timber merchant, managing the family firm in Schaerbeek, a majority Muslim commune in Brussels. He heads up an inter-faith study programme, called the Avicenna Project, which promotes dialogue about the European Union between different religious and humanist traditions—part of the EU initiative *A Soul for Europe*. Jean-Mathieu is a good friend. He does everything with zest. He's no respecter of persons. I've told him I'd like to make him an honorary Protestant! The rough off-white cassock he's wearing now, as he sits beside the others round the table, suits him well.

'Induction ... what does that mean?' the sister introducing the service has a Spanish accent. 'It's not a question of being installed comfortably so as not to move any more. Don't worry, we won't let him get installed like that! Nor does he intend that to happen either. Quite simply, Jean-Mathieu will accompany us in our projects, in our prayer. We will become partners ... The nomination of Jean-Mathieu is the result of a dialogue between the bishop, the dean and the pastoral team. We have met on several occasions. They have listened to us and today are responding to our request.'

She continues in her *midi* accent: 'In this dialogue we want to see the sign of a church we would like to contribute to in our own way—a church which would be the tissue of multiple communities respectful of their differences, a church where we endeavour to share responsibilities, where everyone feels welcome and encouraged, a church open to other cultures and traditions, a church in solidarity with the poor, the marginal, the excluded and those who are united in the struggle for a future of justice and peace.' Her words sound more and more like a confession of faith.

In response, the dean reads the episcopal letter of Jean-Mathieu's nomination. The liturgy unfolds. The Old Testament reading comes from Micah 6, 'What does the Lord require of you but to do justice, to love kindness, and to walk humbly with your God?'; the Epistle from Romans 12, on the diversity of gifts in the body of Christ. A lay woman announces the Gospel—and the lights fuse, leaving the church in semi-darkness! (This is a fairly regular occurrence which takes about ten minutes to fix.) She moves over to a candle and continues, reading Matthew 15: 21-28, the story of the Canaanite woman whose persistence and faith persuaded Jesus to change his mind and heal her tormented daughter. This is followed by silence, after which several members of the congregation comment on the texts. A symbolic action is then introduced—those who so wish are to come forward, take a stone from a basket and place it on the table as a sign of their own particular gift to the community.

The priest of the Romanian Orthodox congregation which uses a side chapel of the church for its worship, is sitting behind us. He takes the opportunity for a quick nap, his thick overcoat bracing him upright in the low kneeling chair. His faint snoring adds a peaceful natural rhythm to the liturgy.

All around people get up and come forward, some in silence, others speaking briefly about what their stones represent. One brings the gift of listening, another her grief about injustice, another contributes the work she does with prostitutes in the neighbourhood. Francette offers the support of a national group called *Soif* (Thirst) which organises sessions on church and society issues. Antoine, a worker priest who lost a hand in an industrial accident, adds a stone he has carried in his pocket for some time. I put a pebble on the pile as a Protestant contribution to this ecumenical Catholic community. Meanwhile the children who are there have, for their part, been drawing pictures to illustrate the theme, and these are now held up for everyone to see.

Jean-Mathieu draws the action to a close with a reference to the Holy Spirit as the mortar which cements these stones together. As the children bring in the elements, we sing a song accompanied by

Andean flutes and guitar: *Je crois en Dieu qui chante,/ et qui fait chanter la vie*, followed by the words of institution, and the sharing of the peace. For the communion, four baskets and chalices are placed at the four corners of the table and we queue up to help ourselves, sipping from a goblet or dipping the crusty wafer in the wine. The dean seems to take it all in his stride. 'Just because he was there for the installation,' Geneviève tells me afterwards, 'we weren't going to celebrate in a more formal way than usual. We did it the way we always do!'

As soon as we leave the circle of the celebration, the cold makes itself felt again. The fiery angels are dragged down the nave to warm up another cluster of adults and children who have already begun sharing a *verre d'amitié*. The drink gives us time to talk; to hear the latest news about *Soif*; to discuss with a friend in the European Commission his complaint that the church has too much influence inside his unit; for Jean-Mathieu to apologise (again!) for the sculpture of St Dominic and the Moor.

Fifty years ago, Cardinal Suhard, the Archbishop of Paris, in a Lenten pastoral which laid the theological foundations for the post-war movement of worker priests in France, said that it was 'a good thing that priests should become witnesses again, less to conquer than to be a sign. This means so to live that one's life would be inexplicable if God did not exist ... Their work is not an excuse or an opportunity for propaganda but an act of naturalisation among people for whom the priest was previously a stranger.'[2]

Today's Brussels *Béguinage* community has quite superseded the identification of the Church with the person of the priest. But Suhard's luminous theology shines through its corporate life as it embraces the mystery of establishing a 'community of destiny with the disinherited'. Squatting in the imposing structure of an empty church, this little congregation bears witness to the Word of God in modern society. Modest Christians though they are, they demonstrate their determination 'to keep the mystery of God present' in an alien world. And their 'sharing of the human lot' is transfigured in celebration.

---

[2] 'The Priest in the Modern World (1949)', in Gregor Siefer, *The Church and Industrial Society*, Darton, Longman and Todd, London, 1964, p. 48.

The story of the greatest miracle

Why, at the dawn of the new era, the very beginning of the fratricidal twentieth century, was I given the name Nadezhda [Hope]?[1]

There is a passage in Dostoevsky's *Crime and Punishment* where the protagonist, Raskolnikov, after committing his dreadful murder, visits a friend called Sonia Marmeladov. Through the poverty and destitution of her family, she has been forced into prostitution. It is late in the evening as he makes his way to her lodgings in St Petersburg in a house by the Ekaterina Canal and she invites him in. Her room is large and sparsely furnished, and dark. They talk by the light of a single candle. Sonia is frightened by Raskolnikov's strange behaviour. Both of them, like so many of Dostoevsky's characters, inhabit a complex, hyper-sensitive region between sanity and madness. Walking excitedly around the room, he picks up an old leather-bound book from the dresser and realises that it is a New Testament. He asks her where she got it and she, quite unaware of the irony in her reply, tells him that Lisaveta gave it to her. Now Lisaveta was the old pawnbroker whom Raskolnikov has just murdered.

'Where is the story of Lazarus?' Raskolnikov asks Sonia, and when she has found the place he tells her to read. 'What for?' she whispers, 'you don't believe.' But he insists, 'Read! I want you to. You used to read to Lisaveta.'

So, with great difficulty, she begins reading the story of the raising of Lazarus. She reads as though she were making a public confession of faith, and as she approaches what Dostoevsky calls 'the story of the greatest miracle', she begins to tremble. Raskolnikov realises that what she is reading she knows by heart. As she reaches the end of the story and closes the Bible, the novel continues, 'She still trembled feaverishly. The candle-end was flickering out in the battered

---

[1] Nadezhda Mandelstam, *Hope against Hope—A Memoir*, trans. Max Hayward, Collins, London, 1971, p. 211.

candlestick, dimly lighting up in the poverty-stricken room the murderer and the harlot who had so strangely been reading together the eternal book.'[2]

I was studying a map of St Petersburg in the library of the Russian Christian Institute in a ground-floor flat on Voznessenki Prospekt when it dawned on me that the house I could see through the window directly across the canal from where I was sitting must be the house where, according to the story, Raskolnikov and Sonia met that night. Dostoevsky wrote about the real Petersburg, as he called the city. Another storey had been added to the house, and the renovated plaster work had been painted a deep yellow, instead of the green in *Crime and Punishment*, but its position made it unmistakable—at the corner of a wide-angled junction of two streets by what is now called the Griboïedova Canal.

I made a pilgrimage to several of the places in the city associated with Dostoevsky—some of the houses he lived in, the streets and gardens where he located characters and events in his novels, the cafe where he joined the radical Petrashevsky circle which was to lead to his being condemned to death, the Peter and Paul Fortress where he was imprisoned, the square where the sham execution took place before he was banished to Siberia.

In the Summer Garden, where Prince Myshkin wandered before his first epileptic fit, a man introduced himself to me as a poet, speaking impeccable French, and inviting me to join him for a literary soirée. *'Je cherche à traduire la musique française en russe,'* he told me. Since the time of Peter the Great and the foundation of the city, St Petersburg has been promoted as a window towards Europe.

Jean-Mathieu, my Belgian friend, had insisted that I buy flowers for Dostoevsky's grave, so I shared the cost of a large bunch of red roses and took them in the name of both of us to the cemetery of Our Lady of Tikhvin. There is a bust of the novelist on the monument over his grave. I laid the flowers beneath it. Tchaikovsky is buried nearby.

The cemetery is off the Alexander Nevsky Square, where the long sweep of the Nevsky Prospekt ends with the Alexander Nevsky Monastery. Founded by Peter the Great in 1710 in honour of the

---

[2] Fyodor Dostoevsky, *Crime and Punishment*, trans. Constance Garnett, The Modern Library, New York, 1950, Part 4, chapter 4, p. 284ff.

saint and national hero who defeated the Swedes, the monastery received the title of 'Lavra' (laureate) held by only three other Russian Orthodox monasteries (one of them in Kiev), and related to their being the seats of metropolitans and church academies. When I visited the Leningrad Academy in 1979, the great Cathedral of the Holy Trinity next door was used as a municipal warehouse! Now it was full of the bustle of baboushkas and the sounds and smells of Orthodox worship. Because of the poor lighting and the grime of candle smoke it was difficult to make out the icons. The relics of Alexander Nevsky were brought back to the cathedral in 1989, though their silver casket is still in the Hermitage.

*   *   *

André Malraux described Rembrandt as 'Dostoevsky's brother, haunted by God'. The extraordinary Rembrandt collection in the Hermitage Museum gives one the chance to reflect on the comparison. There are thirty-six of his paintings, representing many different periods of his life. *Saskia as Flora* dates from 1634, the year of his marriage to Saskia, when he was 28 years old. The *Sacrifice of Abraham* dates from the following year; *David and Jonathan,* from 1641-42, the year of Saskia's death; and the *Holy Family,* 1645. The *Return of the Prodigal Son* was painted in 1668-69, the last year of his life.

The *Prodigal Son* was unfinished when Rembrandt died; the three shadowy figures in the background were completed by another hand. The prodigal kneels, his back towards us, clasping his father's waist. The father is old and frail, but his hands, wide open, rest with infinite tenderness on his son's shoulders and back. 'Rembrandt's prodigal has been broken by his journey from transgression to atonement,' writes Simon Schama. 'The soles of his feet are lacerated and pierced, so that we understand that he has hobbled painfully home towards atonement. His finery hangs in pathetic rags and tatters from his emaciated frame. His head is shorn like a penitent's as he kneels in contrition. We can scarcely make out his features, so lightly has the artist drawn them, but we see enough to know this prodigal for Everyman, for the child who has taken all the sins of the world on his shoulders.'[3] The prodigal son, and indeed the homeless young man

---

[3] Simon Schama, *Rembrandt's Eyes*, Allen Lane, The Penguin Press, London, 1999 p. 658.

who cannot find the way home to his father's house, is the central figure of Dostoevsky's vision.

I visited the Hermitage a second time; my conference included a guided tour. Our guide was a retired art restorer, Mr Alexei Brjancev, who had worked all his life in the Hermitage. A small, lively man, aged 75, his face lit up when speaking about the treasures that had surrounded him all his life. He introduced us to the exquisite collection of Scythian art including the small golden bas relief of a stag, dating from the sixth century BC, which serves as the emblem of the museum; the Raphael Loggias, with all fifty-two subjects from the Old and New Testament reproduced exactly by a team of artists from the originals in the Vatican. And he took us to three galleries where for the first time in half a century a collection of seventy-five paintings, mostly French Impressionists, was on display. These were the paintings taken by the Soviet army as war booty from private collections in Germany at the end of the Second World War. For many years our guide had been one of the curators who inspected the collection in the cellars every few months to ensure that it was in good condition. He was overjoyed to see how beautifully preserved they were now that they were on public display, though the political wrangling over their return to Germany was gaining momentum.

*   *   *

The Russian Museum in St Petersburg was the first museum in Russia to be opened to the public, in 1898. After the revolution of 1917 art works from many other places, including palaces, private collections, cathedrals and churches, were added to its collection. Spanning almost a thousand years of Russian art, from twelfth century icons up to the present times, the collection is so enormous that only a small part of it is on display at any one time. Recently two other palaces in the vicinity were acquired to house parts of the collection.

There is one particularly unusual icon in the Russian Museum which demands special attention. It is of the Novgorod school, early fifteenth century, measuring a large 103 x 77 cm, divided into four quarters, with traditional biblical scenes of Orthodox iconography in each section: *The Resurrection of Lazarus* (top left), *The Hospitality of Abraham*—sometimes called *The Old Testament Trinity*—Abraham and Sarah and their three guests (top right), *The Presentation of Jesus in the*

Temple (bottom left), and *Saint John the Theologian dictating the Good News to his disciple Prochorus* (bottom right). In the museum there are many examples of individual icons on these themes. Why, however, are these four icons included in one work and juxtaposed in this order?

The French philosopher of art, Philippe Sers, confronts this question with the conviction that the icon has a meaning, even though it is not yet understood. 'Access to meaning comes,' Sers writes, 'when one ceases to consider the order of icons as a simple sub-product to illustrate discourse.'[4] It is impossible to confront the icon's mystery without the search for meaning, and the search for meaning in this case makes it necessary to abandon chronological coherence. The clue he finds is in the fact that there is a scroll, representing the Gospel, in three of the icons. Prochorus is writing the Good News in a scroll as Saint John dictates it. In the Hospitality of Abraham, the angel in the middle of the trinity, whose halo is cruciform, therefore representing the Christ, is holding a rolled up scroll in his hand. In the Presentation of Jesus in the Temple, the prophetess Anna has an open scroll in her hand. But there is no scroll in the icon of Lazarus; his resurrection in itself is a foretaste of the resurrection of Jesus. These clues lead Sers to the conclusion that the order in which one must place the four icons, if we wish to understand their meaning, is: *Saint John the Theologian dictating the Good News* (bottom right), *The Hospitality of Abraham* (top right), *The Presentation of Jesus in the Temple* (bottom left), and *The Resurrection of Lazarus* (top left). The presence of the scroll, the Good News, gives meaning and coherence to the whole: first, the Gospel of John being written, then the witness of the Old and New Testaments in chronological order; and finally the resurrection of Lazarus.

In Russian spirituality, the raising of Lazarus is the essential story and the essential icon for the inculturation of the Gospel in society and world.

*   *   *

It was Palm Sunday according to the Orthodox Calendar. The liturgy of the service we attended was in Old Slavonic. Along with the rest of the congregation we were sprinkled with water from willow branches,

---

[4] Philippe Sers, *L'énigme de l'icône quadripartite de Saint-Pétersbourg,* La Lettre volée, Bruxelles, 1996, p. 5.

and on leaving were given some pussy willow twigs to take with us. It was snowing again when we left the chapel, as if Spring had forgotten St Petersburg this year.

I am Švejk

The drama which is playing in Prague is not of a local nature …
it reflects in a very concentrated way the destiny of Europe. What
is playing in Prague is the grand, tragic drama of European illusions
and follies; what is being anticipated in Prague is the possible ruin
of Europe. That's the reason why the least Czech is a much more
convinced European than any Frenchman or Dane. For he sees
'Europe dying' every day with his own eyes, and every day he is
obliged to defend 'the Europe that is in him'.[1]

Karlův Most, the Charles Bridge, was not always so called after the
Bohemian King and Holy Roman Emperor, Charles IV. For long enough
it was the only bridge across the Vltava, known as Prague Bridge or
simply The Bridge. During the golden age of art and architecture in
the fourteenth century, when the first university of the Empire was
being founded and St Vitus Cathedral built, Charles had it reconstructed.
Since then it has been called the Charles Bridge linking the *Malá Strana*
and the *Staré Mesto*, the Lesser City and the Old Town of Prague, at
the crossroads of central Europe.

What Ivo Andrić writes in *The Bridge over the Drina* about the
sixteenth century bridge the Turks built over the river dividing Serbia
and Bosnia-Herzegovina, describes the Charles Bridge just as well.
'The significance and substance of its existence were, so to speak, in
its permanence. Its shining line in the composition of the town did not
change, any more than the outlines of the mountains against the sky.
In the changes and the quick burgeoning of human generations, it
remained as unchanged as the waters that flowed beneath it. It grew
old, naturally, but on a scale of time that was much greater not only
than the span of human existence but also than the passing of a whole
series of generations, so that its ageing could not be seen by human
eye. Its life, though mortal in itself, resembled eternity for its end
could not be perceived.'[2]

---

[1] Milan Kundera, *Le Nouvel Observateur*, November 1979, my translation.

[2] Ivo Andrić, *The Bridge over the Drina*, trans. Lovett F Edwards, Harville, London, 1994, p.71.

Unlike the bridge over the Drina and another ancient bridge, the bridge at Mostar, which were eventually destroyed by men at war, the Charles Bridge has been wonderfully preserved. Five hundred metres long, ten metres wide, its sixteen arches provide ample shelter for pigeons, seagulls, ducks and lovers. Battles have been fought on its broad back, blood shed on its cobbled pavement. Motor cars drove across it between the wars. Over the centuries it has served as market place and meeting place, jousting ground and gallow land, long before it became today's pop art mart and tourist rendezvous.

If you stand in the middle of the Charles Bridge under the worn stone sculpture of St Christopher and the Christ child bearing the world, and look back towards the old town, above the Old Town Tower's gothic saints and emperors, you can see a statue of Atlas supporting the heavens. I daresay it's the only place in Europe where public monuments of these two mythical giants of our civilisation are visible at the same time.

The St Christopher is one of thirty religious statues that line the bridge, dating mostly from the eighteenth century. The Atlas tops the astronomers' tower of the Clementinum, a vast cluster of churches and chapels, courtyards, classrooms, libraries, residences and refectories, built as a university college by the Jesuits. Thirty-two burghers' houses were demolished to make room for its construction. Today it accommodates several of the city's libraries. Tourists are not allowed, but in 1965 when visitors from the west were rare, my friend Josef asked the porter if he would show me the observatory. And he obliged. A gentle, ageing anarchist, he climbed the high staircase with us to the top. The slender tower rises beside the baroque domes of the St Clement and St Salvator churches in the complex. Completed in 1723, it houses an observatory with ancient astronomical instruments and is topped by the life-sized lead statue of the titan Atlas.

When Anne of Bohemia, the daughter of Charles IV, married Richard II of England in 1383, many Czech students went to Oxford to study. They came under the influence of John Wycliffe and brought his teachings back to Prague, so encouraging the reform movement in the Czech lands. Jan Hus was a follower of Wycliffe, though his way of combining religious and patriotic zeal was peculiarly Bohemian. The first martyr to the reformed faith in Scotland was a Czech, Pavel Crawar, burnt at the stake in St Andrews in 1433, nearly a century before the death of Patrick Hamilton, the first Scottish martyr, and years before John Knox was even born. 'We are all of us Hussites without knowing it,' Luther wrote in 1529.

The Austrian Archduke Ferdinand I coveted the throne of Bohemia, and finally got himself elected to it in 1526. So, while the Reformation was in full swing elsewhere in Europe, the Hapsburgs brought the Jesuits to Prague to spearhead the Counter-Reformation. The Czech reform movement was very nearly extinguished.

There is a map of Europe, published in Prague in 1537, which depicts the continent in the form of a Queen, the Virgin Mary, representing the Catholic faith. I found a map dealer once in the Golden Lane behind the cathedral, who had an original, but he wouldn't part with it. In the stylized etching, seas and rivers, mountain ranges, cities, states and regions define and adorn the Virgin's figure. The Iberian peninsula is her head with Lusitania and Hispania inscribed on her crown. Navarre and Aragon are the names on her hair. Her breast and shoulders are Gallia and France; Denmark is one arm and Italy the other, holding Sicily as an orb. She wears a medallion round her neck with Bohemia on it and a cameo of the steeples and domes of Prague. Her regal skirts follow a straightened seam of the Danube to the Black Sea. Constantinople and Moscow are in her train.

Europe as the Virgin Queen is a starkly monocultural representation of Europe, an attempt to state and reinstate the hegemony of the Catholic Church. The efforts of the Roman Catholic Church today to regain its former property, confiscated in 1948, should come as no surprise. There are four hundred current claims on churches, ecclesiastical institutions, farms and forests in the Czech Republic.

The Czech people finally revolted against Ferdinand II in 1618. Their defeat at the Battle of the White Mountain marked the start of the Thirty Years' War. The century and a half which followed is called the 'Age of Darkness'. Czech religious and national liberty was lost for three hundred years. And even then, Tomáš Masaryk's republic of 1918 lasted for only twenty years, to be followed by Nazi occupation, Communist putsch and Soviet normalisation.

*   *   *

It was late one evening in the summer of 1965 that I arrived in Prague for the first time. The doorbell at the former bakery in Belohorská, up behind the castle, didn't work and, in spite of the little group of passers-by who stopped to help me, throwing pebbles at the windows of the flat above the shop, my arrival went unnoticed inside. An old lady took me home for the night, fed me well and brought me back after breakfast to find my friend Josef. He's now living there again but in a completely renovated flat. His father's properties, confiscated by the Communists in 1948, including the flat over the bakery where he and his mother were allowed to stay, have been returned. For twenty-five years Joe worked as a water engineer. He earns his living now as a tourist guide and landlord of his few rented properties. He would have preferred to be a businessman, but it's too late now. Like several of my Czech friends he suffers from depression.

Supper at Vlastá's—bottled plums in cream cheese dumplings with melted butter, icing sugar and ground poppyseed. Vlastá was the most constant feature of our visits to Prague in the decades which followed. The generosity she showed us, for one who had so little. She was a constant reference concerning the political perversity of post-war Czechoslovakia and the hypocrisies of normalisation. She offered a critique of our socialist idealism, and provided a touchstone for the struggles of a church freed from what the theologian Josef Hromádka called its 'Constantinian captivity', only to be plunged into a different kind of ideological dilemma.

At the end of a visit in 1975 to Teleci, the Moravian village where our friend Tomáš was pastor, he said to me in his wry way, 'Next time we meet I'll be a member of the ruling class.' And he was right. His involvement in Charter 77 led to the loss of his pastor's licence. He became a forester, a worker. Eventually, with Daniela his wife and their four children, they came into exile in Scotland. Now back in Prague, he has obtained a copy of his secret police file during those years. 'The object,' it reads (he is referred to as 'the object' throughout), 'the object was visited in his manse by Hulbert who asked the object to give information about the church political situation and offered him large sums of money from Radio Free Europe!'

Svát'a too was a signatory of Charter 77, a sixties radical who lost his licence soon after normalisation began. In the early seventies he was writing songs based on Bible stories and singing them in his own wild, urgent way. He helped form the pop group, Plastic People, which played all over the country, in pubs and railway trains, at secret trysts and weddings in the woods. Employed as a window cleaner in

159

Prague, he was much in demand, not so much to clean windows as to minister to alienated youngsters in the underground. Couples sought him out to baptise their children. When a young conscript hanged himself, his friends asked Svát'a to take the funeral.

He was imprisoned regularly, on the slightest pretext, for a day or two—at the anniversary of the Warsaw Pact invasion, at the trial of the spokesmen of Charter 77, on May 1—to keep him out of the way! By the end of the seventies he couldn't take it any more. His whole family was suffering. They left for Vienna and he was offered a job with the church in Zürich where there was a large Czech exile community.

Svát'a is back in Prague now as minister of St Salvator's, a large protestant church near the Old Town Square. His preaching, I am told, is deep and poetic. This Sunday an evangelical student choir from Philadelphia in the USA was to sing at the service. We just happened to be there, Josef and I, and since there was no one else, Joe acted as interpreter. St Salvator's is a tall gothic church that was not reoccupied by the Catholics after the Reformation, its plane walls and simple furnishings in stark contrast to the heavy baroque marble and the gilded woodwork of so many of Prague's Catholic churches. The young Americans' jazz and gospel songs were much appreciated.

After the service was over, the choir stayed behind to hear Svát'a's story. A student asked him to sing one of his songs, and after a moment's hesitation, he went off to fetch a guitar. The song he sang was the title song of a record from 1977, his version of a negro spiritual, *Say No to the Devil*. The chorus was in English. 'One should learn to recognise the source of evil,' he told them, 'the forms it appears in. Evil can mask itself so well.' These kids were not born in 1968. They knew nothing about Marxism and the history of Communism in Europe, about the Prague Spring or Charter 77. But they loved this aging hippy with his long hair and wispy beard who sang passionately about the enemy: 'The devil is a deceiver,/he don't treat nobody right … Say no to the devil,/say no …'

In *Summer Meditations*, Václav Havel writes: 'Every European country has something particular to it—and that makes its autonomy worth defending, even in the framework of an integrating Europe. That autonomy then enriches the entire European scene; it is another voice in that remarkable polyphony, another instrument in that orchestra. And I feel that our historical experience, our intellectual and spiritual potential, our experience of misery, absurdity, violence, and idyllic tranquillity, our humour, our experience of sacrifice, our love of civility, our love of truth and our knowledge of the many ways truth can be betrayed—all this can, if we wish, create another of those distinct voices from which the chorus of Europe is composed.'[3]

The way Svát'a spoke to the American students reminded me of a text in the Book of Deuteronomy, 'When your children ask you in time to come, What is the meaning of these things? then you shall say to them, We were slaves in Pharaoh's Egypt ...' He was telling these 'children' what it meant to live under Communism and struggle against it. He was bearing witness to the truth as it had been in a time of falsehood. So much of what Havel calls 'our historical experience, our intellectual and spiritual potential' of the last half-century in Eastern Europe is despised, disregarded, disqualified by the brash new global culture of the West. And it continues to be.

Svát'a finished singing, looked at his watch and announced that he had to go. He was officiating at a wedding that afternoon in a forest in southern Bohemia.

After lunch with Joe I wandered through the streets of Prague alone and called in at the National Gallery's St Agnes Convent. Adolf Kosárek, a young painter in 1848, the year of revolutions, fell in love and was engaged when he discovered he was suffering from tuberculosis. He died at the age of 29, but only after completing some vivid landscape paintings. The turmoil in his heart is perhaps best understood in *The Country Wedding*, a sombre picture completed shortly before his death. A colourful peasant wedding party—bride, groom, brass band and guests in two sturdy horse-drawn wagons, accompanied by men on horseback—rides at the gallop through a deserted, rocky valley. The wild sense of urgency struggles with the sense of celebration in a landscape full of foreboding.

*   *   *

Travelling along a road in spreading darkness
whose chill stretches away into the trees;

---

[3] Václav Havel, *Summer Meditations*, trans. Paul Wilson, Faber and Faber, London, 1992, p. 127.

travelling in between grey mounds of snow
which slowly thaw into the mists of winter is no more.

'The road from Amberg to Pilsen,' you said, turning to me in the car (it was Easter 1997), 'hasn't changed much from when we did it in March 1970. Apart from the night-clubs and brothels that have sprung up on the Czech side. There's the same dirty snow, the same grey villages, the same feeling of weariness everywhere. It must have looked like this after the war. … It's after a war now, the Cold War. So much destruction: houses, farms, public buildings … most of all, people's lives!'

'Next morning in church at Mladá Boleslav,' I said, 'you were speaking at the service and Freddie was helping you with your Czech. You couldn't stop crying, thinking of the Prague Spring and what had happened since August '68. But Freddie understood. He would laugh a little and shrug things off. It was the same even after he lost his licence and became a stoker …'

'We artists lost in the revolution,' Michál Kocáb said in a BBC documentary called 'Absurdistan'. Michál was Freddie's son, composer and rock musician, then MP and Minister of State supervising the Soviet withdrawal from Czech territory after the Velvet Revolution. 'We all lost maybe more than the Communists, since our lifelong work was focused directly on criticising the regime. We knew the ropes and now we're in the position of grumbling slaves, who, having spent seventy years being whipped daily somewhere on a sugar cane plantation, were suddenly taken to Paris. And the slave misses his milieu, the environment where he'd learned to live.'

Under Communism officially there was no unemployment, but many people had meaningless jobs. As the century ends, how many beautiful young people do meaningless jobs under the astronomical clock in the Old Town Square, dressed up as Mozart, Don Giovanni or Donna Elvira, handing out publicity for operas and concerts, selling many-coloured hats, stained-glass flowers, wind-up birds, jumping spiders, squawking hens, spinning tops, Russian dolls, potato pancakes, rye bread and sausages? You get the feeling in Prague that it's all happened before, that—like the bridge—'the significance and substance of its existence [are], so to speak, in its permanence.'

After a performance of Mozart's *Requiem* in the Bethlehem Chapel where Jan Hus used to preach six hundred years ago, I watched the tympanist, an old man, carry his kettle drums out of the church one by one and pack them carefully into his ageing, chocolate brown Trabant van. For all the changes in society and the quickening pace of life, it takes the same time to play Mozart's *Requiem* today as it did when it was first performed in Prague in the decade following the French Revolution.

A few years after the First World War Jaroslav Hašek wrote, 'Today you can meet in the streets of Prague a shabbily dressed man who is not even himself aware of his significance in the history of the great new era. He goes modestly on his way without bothering anyone. Nor is he bothered by journalists asking for an interview. If you asked him his name he would answer you simply and unassumingly: I am Švejk …'[4]

---

[4] Jaroslav Hašek, *The Good Soldier Švejk*, trans. Cecil Parrott, Penguin Books, London, 1973, p. 1.

North wind blowing, blowing hard

*Dans tous les pays du monde, ne sommes-nous pas condamnés à
rechercher l'île peu frequenté pour y retrouver non la gloire, mais la
paix d'un paradis que nous sommes sûr d'avoir perdu?*[1]

Five in the morning and the night ferry from Mykonos glided into
Skala bay, the port of the Isle of Patmos. I stood in the stern watching
the stars in the night sky, the slenderest of waning moons, and the
great constellation of Orion dipping towards the horizon.

A couple of aged monks, one nun, three sleepy tourists and
me—along with some bags and packages—were all the big ship had to
deliver before she was off again to her next port of call. I picked my
way along the coast road southwards in the direction of the village of
Grikos until, round the promontory on the far side of the bay, the
horizon to the east came obscurely into view. There was a low stone
jetty jutting into the sea below the bluff where the road ran, and I sat
myself down on it to await the dawn.

The surface of the water was limpid calm. An occasional fish
jumped in the dark. When it was light enough I could distinguish many
zig-zag lines cutting the delicate meniscus of the inlet by which I sat. It
was a shoal of little fish, their mouths open to catch insects, tracing
lines across the surface of the water. Two early, unkempt crows flew
overhead and perched in a nearby tree, croaking hoarsely to each
other as if they shared a hang-over. A cock crew somewhere behind
me. The first fishing boat out of Skala, hardly distinguishable but for
its lights, disturbed the stillness with the distant chug-chug of its engine
and the Orthodox liturgy on its radio. A man in a rowing boat, its bows
low in the water, stern high (he was sitting so far forward), headed for
the open sea. Like the blinded Orion in the ancient story rowing towards
the farthest ocean if only Helius, the Sun, might restore his sight.

---

[1] In all the countries of the world, are we not condemned to seek for a quiet little
island so as to rediscover not the glory, but the peace of a paradise that we are sure to
have lost?
Fernand Braudel, my translation.

Seated on my jetty, bare feet in the sea, I watched Orion sidle down the sky and Dawn rise to greet him. *Eos*, Dawn, was married to *Astraeus*, the Dawn Wind; it was she who gave birth to the Morning Star and the other winds, North, South and West. But she had many lovers besides her husband, and as everyone knew Orion was the handsomest man alive. She invited him to her couch on the holy isle of Delos. She still blushes at her indiscretion. I no doubt blushed to watch her then. For all my concentration, the sunrise surprised me with its sudden beauty: the first brilliant sliver of silver breasting the low isle of Lipsi, the speed with which the golden orb rose to reveal its full glory, the reflected light on the brazen sea as the sky lit up another day.

I rented a room in the garden of a shopkeeper's house in Skala. Autumn was in the evening wind rustling the leaves of the pomegranate tree before my door, blowing purple and orange petals from the bougainvillea along the pathway. In the morning sun a friendly cat sat with me while I ate my breakfast and caressed my legs with its warm fur.

Patmos is about eight miles long, its narrow waist just north of Skala only a few hundred yards wide. I set off at dawn one day for Lambi in the north where the beach is famous for its many coloured stones. They are piled up all along the foreshore, beautiful, yet different from the stones and pebbles at Columba's Bay, Iona, which are constantly moving with the sea. The movement of the tide at Lambi is negligible. In the afternoon I made my way to the secluded sandy beach of Psili Ammos in the south and swam naked for an hour in the huge waves rolling in from the open sea.

The islands of the Dodecanese are more fertile than the Cyclades, though water is not plentiful on Patmos. Patmos has a variety of trees, native and imported—pine, fir, cyprus, eucalyptus, alder, a species of rowan, pear, pomegranate, almond, olive, fig, and others I didn't know the names of. I watched a goatherd lead his goats across a rocky pasture shouting and whistling at them all the while, tossing stones this way and that to keep them together. After my swim I climbed the peak of Kouvari to watch the sun set behind Mykonos sixty miles away. The light was 'thickening' as another goatherd in a field drew bucket after bucket from a well to water his thirsty flock.

You don't have to be long in the Greek islands to get a feel for Homer's epithets to describe the natural world:

the broad-backed sea
the spacious, barren, billowing, loud-moaning sea
the whitening, blue-glancing, wine-dark sea
  —and the lovely lake of ocean

the arching heaven
mysterious, sable night

Dawn of the braided tresses
Dawn in her flowery garment
Dawn of the broidered robe, the golden robes
  —coming early, with rosy fingers

white-armed Nausicaa
white-armed girls or nymphs
  —whose loveliness is the graces' gift

sweet wine
wine which coils its way round the understanding

sleep—
delicious, unbroken, care-charming sleep
sleep that soothes limbs and anxious hearts
sleep to cover the eyelids over
with quick release from toil and pain

man—most frail
of all things that breathe and move on earth
heart-withering anguish
  —men have but a short time to live

I was reading Homer's *Odyssey*[2] (in a fine translation by Walter Shewring) for the first time since I was at school. Robert Graves' *Greek Myths*[3] was my other companion. A week later in the library of the Orthodox Academy on Crete I came across these words in an old book on Christian symbolism: 'There was hardly an object in the

---

[2] Homer, *The Odyssey*, trans. Walter Shewring, OUP, Oxford, 1980.
[3] Robert Graves, *op. cit.*

kingdom of Nature which did not form part of the symbolism of the early Christians, who looked upon the whole outward world as a mirror wherein were reflected the higher truths of the invisible kingdom, and as symbolic of Salvation through Christ.' Classical or Christian, nature is incorporated into art in wonderful ways.

*   *   *

The Monastery of St John the Divine dominates the hilltop town of Chora like a crusader fortress. Its high, limestone walls and buttresses tower over the white-washed houses clustered round it. Inside, the courtyard walls, passageways and flat roofs are also brilliant white. It was built at the same time as St Andrews Cathedral, and the Sainte Chapelle on the Île de France in Paris, where the rose window illustrates the drama of the Apocalypse in much greater detail than the Orthodox icons of Patmos. Almost a millennium of devotion has bequeathed the Monastery of St John with treasures of exquisite beauty: parchment manuscripts, woven vestments, ecclesiastical furnishings, gold and silver vessels, frescos and icons.

Most beautiful of all is the Chapel of the Virgin, which flanks the north side of the church. Tremors from an earthquake which struck Santorini forty years ago dislodged the plasterwork of the mediocre 18th century wall-paintings that used to decorate the little chapel. The original 12th century Byzantine frescos which were thus exposed and then restored are the oldest of their kind to survive in Greece. Scenes from the healing miracles of the gospels adorn the walls—the ten lepers, blind Bartemaeus, the paralytic, the woman with the haemorrhage. Above the apse, on the east wall, is the Hospitality of Abraham, the Orthodox symbol of the Trinity. Beneath it, behind the early 17th century wooden iconostasis, is a fresco of the Virgin Enthroned with Angels. The Virgin holds the Christ child on her lap. On either side of her majestic throne stand the Archangels Michael and Gabriel, bearing banners, dressed in the raiment of the Byzantine imperial guard, wings folded. The sombre colours of the painting—dark red, deep blue, blue-grey, black, white, crimson, gold—the austerity of the composition, the nobility of the saints' frontal pose, their solemn looks and formidable, watchful eyes, combine to give the fresco an overwhelming power. It made me weep. A reminder of the root force of Christendom in the old stock of Europe. What could not regular devotion to such an icon do to the human spirit? Till the day I die I shall remember the look of that woman and her son and their two heavenly guards watching me, watching over me.

At the end of my final visit to the Monastery (I went several times), coming out under the great arched doorway at the top of the ramp that mounts the eastern fortifications, I stopped to gaze one last time at the panorama before me. It was September 1, the evening of the first day of autumn, Creation Day in the new Orthodox calander.

The land falls away steeply from that point. You look down past the pleasant jumble of Chora's white-washed houses, over the road the island bus toils up four times a day, out into a huge, wide, terraced amphitheatre of rough grass, scrub bushes, dry stone walls and sparse groves of olive and almond trees, that sweeps down by the buttressed walls of the Grotto of the Apocalypse to the port of Scala. Beyond Skala bay, the island stretches north towards Samos across the sea with its bald peak of Kerkettos on the horizon. To the east are the islands of Arki and Lipsi; to the south-east, Leros, Kalymnos, Kos, and the rest of the islands of the Dodecanese, like stepping stones to Rhodes. The Venetians called the Aegean Sea the Archipelago. Ancient Ephesus (whence St John was exiled to Patmos) lies to the north-east, and the long coastline of Asia Minor serves as a reminder that the Isle of Patmos lies at the very edge of Europe, at the frontier, where West meets East.

Outside the monastery, the last tourists had clattered away down the cobbles. I stopped, transfixed. The north wind was blowing, blowing hard. Three birds were in the sky (I never found out what they were), playing on the wind, with the wind. Soaring with wings wide spread, diving wings furled, darting here and there with a sudden turn of speed, chasing each another, riding the wind as if to catch their breath, dashing, swerving, stalling, dipping, dropping, tumbling, levelling— beginning all over again. I daresay the melodrama matched the best that ever festivals of Greece or Europe staged! I watched enthralled, and when eventually they disappeared round the side of the hill, I felt bereft. A collared dove settled on an olive branch beside the terrace where I stood and cocked an eye at me as if it noticed the tears in mine. The fierce north wind blew both soon away.

As though the energies of all creation had been mustered for an hour just for me—celestial circus, anarchy in the cosmos, a vision of the Holy Trinity on holiday. Ken Patchen, I thought, you got it right!

Jesus its beautiful
Great mother of big apples its a pretty world

Youre a bastard Mr Death
And I wish you didnt have no look-in here

I dont know how the rest of you feel
But I feel drunk all the time
And I wish to hell we didnt have to die

O youre a merry bastard Mr Death
And I wish you didnt have no hand in this game

One of the birds reappeared for a solo encore that took it spiralling up and up into the mysterious, arching heaven until, although I strained my eyes to see, it vanished into infinity. I went down the hillside in the dark. As I reached the lights of Skala, something blew across my path. I picked it up. It was a 5000 Drachma note—enough to buy a pair of amber ear-rings in the Plaka for my wife!

Iona

More, more than flies in amber

Civilisation begins with names and must end when they end ...
Without names for ourselves and our possessions and places we
return to the void ... If you had a good enough map ... you would
find them. But these are flies in amber.[1]

Well of the North Wind   *Tobar na Gaoithe Tuath*
Island of Storm   *Eilean Annraidh*
          Height of the Storm   *Ard Annraidh*
                    Hill-Fort of Iona   *Dun I*

        I met a man called Peter, surnamed
        Finister, in the Abbey of Iona.
        His great great grandfather was shipwrecked
        years ago off the north-west coast of Spain.
        He was the sole survivor, lost
        his memory with the break-up of the ship.
        English sailors saved his life
        and brought him home to England, called him
        Finisterre, later Finister, after Cape
        Finisterre, where land ends
        in the Atlantic and his ship went down.
        He married an English girl,
        founded a family, made
        a new name.

        Hill of the Oak   *Cnoc Daraich*
    Cliff of the Rowan   *Allt a'Chaorainn*
        Place of Red Flowers   *Ruanaich*
          Enclosure of Thorns   *Garadh Sgelban*

---

[1] Alasdair Maclean, *Night Falls on Ardnamurchan*, Penguin Books, London, 1984, p. 185-6.

At sunrise, leaving by the Abbey door
That leads to the Big Meadow, *Liana Mhor,*
I startled a corncrake in open ground
Where the timid creature's rarely found—
Plump, golden in the morning light,
Wings whirring, but the same desolate cry in flight
As when hidden in its habitat of hay field or wild iris:
Crex crex in Latin, declining species in the Hebrides.

Dell of the Tent	*Glac a' Phubail*
Point of the Height	*Ru' na h'Aird*
Port of Community	*Port na Muinntir*
Point of the Kite	*Ru' a'Chosgarnaich*
Port of the Hermitage	*Port an Diseirt*
Hill of the Well	*Cnoc an Tobair*
Graveyard of Oran	*Reilig Orain*

where the gravestones tell
the names of islanders and kings.

*   *   *

The softest of southerlies over *Dun I*
holds my crimson kite aloft, rippling
like a T-shirt on the wind's back—
Hebridean day of absolute summer:
opalescent sea, lazy haze on the Cuillins,
far, far the view of the Treshnish Isles,
Skye, Coll, Tiree—
           space rooted in place,
           place not in a void,
           yet a place and the space
           for there to be nothing—
deep peace of the emptiness of sea and sky.

The lark sings softly in nature's liturgy.
The gull that shared my bread glides off the hill.
On mossy turf I lie, arms wide
out-stretched to the firmament,
hands holding the lines

171

that hold the kite
that holds—at an observable distance—
    time, space,
    life, place,
    me, nature,
    now.